Japanese Private Economic Diplomacy

William E. Bryant

The Praeger Special Studies program—
utilizing the most modern and efficient book
production techniques and a selective
worldwide distribution network—makes
available to the academic, government, and
business communities significant, timely
research in U.S. and international economic, social, and political development.

Japanese Private Economic Diplomacy

An Analysis of Business-Government Linkages

Praeger Publishers   New York   Washington   London

PRAEGER SPECIAL STUDIES IN INTERNATIONAL POLITICS AND GOVERNMENT

Library of Congress Cataloging in Publication Data

Bryant, William E
    Japanese private economic diplomacy.

    (Praeger special studies in international politics
and government)
    Bibliography: p.
    1. Japan—Foreign economic relations.
2. Businessmen—Japan. I. Title.
HF1601.B78   382'.0952   74-332
ISBN 0-275-09180-5

PRAEGER PUBLISHERS
111 Fourth Avenue, New York, N.Y. 10003, U.S.A.
5, Cromwell Place, London SW7 2JL, England

Published in the United States of America in 1975
by Praeger Publishers, Inc.

Printed in the United States of America

To Mom, Pop, and Jimbo

One of the first discoveries for any student of postwar Japanese government and foreign relations is the primacy in Japan of economic factors under a close business-government relationship. In order to grasp at least a portion of this relationship I wrote an earlier essay on one of the major business associations, "Keizai Doyukai: A Japanese Interest Group," for the Certificate of the East Asian Institute of Columbia University. From it emerged Japanese economic missions as a dissertation topic which would examine the business-government partnership in the context of international relations. During advanced Japanese language study and preliminary research in Tokyo the missions theme was broadened to include other international activities of businessmen—roving ambassadorships, joint economic committees, and international conferences—all of which come under the Japanese label of private economic diplomacy (minkan keizai gaiko).

No analysis of the topic had been published by Western writers; the only Japanese analysis available was the transcript of a roundtable discussion by members of Keidanren (Federation of Economic Organizations) which introduced me to the concept private economic diplomacy and was seminal to the entire study.*

The purpose of the present study is to explore the meaning of that concept, analyzing the linkages between Japanese business and government and between domestic and international politics, taking the individual business leader as the connecting link.

Because of the lack of literature on the topic I conducted interviews in both Japanese and English with businessmen and officials in Japan and surveyed available press and official reports to determine if the distribution and frequency of diplomatic activities by businessmen followed a systematic pattern. If so, I felt, the function of these activities could be defined and evaluated within the overall context of Japanese diplomacy.

The only library adequate for the task proved to be that of Keidanren in Tokyo. I am greatly indebted to Keidanren staff members

---

*Kiichiro Sato et al., "Minkan keizai gaiko no yakuwari to seika" [The role and results of private economic diplomacy], Keidanren Geppo, December 1967, pp. 1-17. An abridged English translation is also available as "The Role of Private Economic Diplomacy," Keidanren Review, No. 8 (March 1968), pp. 26-35.

Katsuhiro Fujiwara, Natsuaki Fusano, Masaya Miyoshi, Kazuo Nukazawa, and Atsuo Ueda who provided much assistance. Tadashi Shishido of Keizai Doyukai (Japan Committee for Economic Development) generously provided data for that business association. Professors Makoto Saito and Taichiro Mitani of the University of Tokyo, and James W. Morley, James I. Nakamura, Gerald L. Curtis, and the late Philip E. Mosely of Columbia University all guided me along the slow path of research, writing, and rewriting.

LIST OF TABLES

LIST OF ABBREVIATIONS

ADB	Asian Development Bank
ADELA	Atlantic Community Development Group for Latin America
BOJ	Bank of Japan
ASEAN	Association of Southeast Asian Nations
ASPAC	Asian and Pacific Council
CACCI	Confederation of Asian Chambers of Commerce and Industry
CBI	Confederation of British Industries
CED	Committee for Economic Development (United States)
CEDA	Committee for Economic Development of Australia
CEMLA	Center for Latin American Monetary Studies (Mexico)
CEPES	Committee for Economic and Social Progress (France, Germany, Italy)
Doyukai	Keizai Doyukai (Japan Committee for Economic Development)
ECAFE	Economic Commission for Asia and the Far East
EEC	European Economic Community (European Common Market)
EPA	Keizai Kikakucho (Economic Planning Agency)
FTC	Kosei Torihiki Iinkai (Fair Trade Commission)
GATT	General Agreement on Tariffs and Trade
IGGI	Intergovernmental Group on Indonesia
IMF	International Monetary Fund

JCA	Japan-California Association
JETRO	Japan Export Trade Organization
Keidanren	Keizai Dantai Rengokai (Federation of Economic Organizations)
LDP	Jiyuminshuto (Liberal Democratic Party)
MITI	Tsusansho (Ministry of International Trade and Industry)
Nikkeiren	Nihon Keieisha Dantai Renmei (Japan Federation of Employers' Organizations)
Nissho	Nihon Shoko Kaigisho (Japan Chamber of Commerce and Industry)
OECD	Organization for Economic Cooperation and Development
PBEC	Pacific Basin Economic Council
PEP	Political and Economic Planning (Great Britain)
PIBA-IPC	Pacific-Indonesia Business Association-Investment Promotion Council
PICA	Private Investment Company for Asia
Sanken	Sangyo Mondai Kenkyukai (Industrial Problems Research Society)
SIE	Seminars for Economic Research (Spain)
SNS	The Industrial Council for Social and Economic Studies (Sweden)
SRI	Stanford Research Institute (United States)
UNCTAD	United Nations Conference on Trade and Development
UNDP	United Nations Development Program

Japanese Private
Economic Diplomacy

1

TOWARD A
MORE FAVORABLE
ECONOMIC CLIMATE

The postwar Japanese businessman has proven his ability many times over, essentially blotting out the old notion that he produced only imitative and mediocre goods. In the process, however, he has acquired in some quarters a reputation as an "economic animal"[1]; and has even yet to establish in the eyes of the world a reputation for interests broader than mere trade and investment.[2] This study concerns one of the means by which Japanese businessmen, in cooperation with government, are attempting to pursue interests that include corporate profits but in a broader context of advancing their country's diplomatic objectives.

Basically, Japan's private economic diplomacy is a systematic effort by business and government to establish a favorable climate for improving economic relations with foreign countries by utilizing businessmen in official and unofficial roles. The businessman may be sent on economic missions sponsored either by government or business; he may travel as a roving ambassador appointed by the foreign minister; he may attend meetings of joint economic committees composed of businessmen from two or more countries, or international businessmen's conferences on trade and policy matters.

One may distinguish missions as government or business sponsored, roving ambassadorships as exclusively governmental, and joint economic committees or conferences as exclusively business sponsored. This study, however, will ignore this distinction on the ground that the source of official sponsorship obscures the fact that these are variant forms of a single activity and that analytical distinctions are more meaningful at the level of groups and individuals within government and business rather than treating government and business as single entities.

The economic mission is the standard vehicle for the purpose of establishing a favorable climate with another country. Once initially established by a mission or roving ambassador, the climate must be maintained against recurring devisive issues. This is done through dispatching subsequent missions or through ongoing joint economic committees and business conferences. The latter two are useful for maintenance purposes because they provide regular channels for communication and can focus on long-term problems.

The choice of which type of diplomacy to use also varies with the particular mix of secondary objectives, which differ for each country or region: (1) improve Japan's popular image abroad; (2) give special attention to selected countries or regions; (3) remove obstacles to trade and investment; (4) negotiate agreements; and (5) gather information and formulate policy recommendations.

An example of how private economic diplomacy is carried out in the case of a government sponsored economic mission is as follows:[3] The Foreign Ministry appoints a businessman as the mission leader after consultation with officers of leading business associations. The leader then selects other members of the mission who must, however, be acceptable to both business and government authorities. Preparatory briefings are held, arrangements are made for the itinerary, and the mission departs for one to four weeks. Advisers from interested Japanese ministries may accompany the mission to ensure that the views presented are informed and consistent with national policy. Upon their return, members of the mission draft a formal report that includes recommendations for follow-up action or new policies. This entails more consultation with government and business leaders in order to arrive at a consensus of views among different ministries, business associations, and individuals.[4] The members' final report is distributed to all interested parties as both an official record and a working paper for further debate and action. It represents a consensus of participating interests, or more accurately, a consensus of business participants with modifying inputs from government.

In this perspective Japan's private economic diplomacy can be considered an extension of domestic politics to the arena of international relations by which two kinds of purposes are served: (1) diplomatic purposes according to official policy for specific countries and regions; and (2) separate purposes of participating groups and individuals, including those of government agencies, business associations, companies, and individual business leaders. For example, one ministry may participate to gain business support vis-a-vis another ministry; businessmen may participate to enhance their careers or to gather support for a particular policy position. Behind the apparent unanimity of a Japanese economic delegation one should look for the constant interplay of internal forces at various points in time and for the bureaucratic hierarchy. This applies to the selection of personnel for the various missions, roving ambassadorships, joint committees and conferences, and during all phases of preparation, execution, and follow-up. In this manner Japan's private economic diplomacy actively supplements professional diplomacy in building a better climate abroad because it also serves to advance diverse underlying interests of government, business, and individual participants.

THE INTERNATIONAL CONTEXT:
HOW DIFFERENT ARE THE JAPANESE?

There is nothing exclusively Japanese about private economic diplomacy; many nations practice it in one form or another, and each mission or joint committee implies a reciprocal initiative. The differences lie in the manner and extent to which the Japanese apply the idea.[5] It is all too easy to look at the differences and characterize the Japanese approach as unique—whether for political, economic, or cultural reasons—as if uniqueness explains everything. But if one digs beneath the overall objective of establishing a favorable climate and asks the question—favorable to whom and for what?—one finds a cluster of cooperating and competing group and individual interests which do not support simplistic notions of a "Japan Incorporated"[6] or a monolithic power elite carrying out a diplomatic grand design under a single national interest.[7] Such concepts put too much stress on the degree of Japanese unanimity and cooperation* while over-looking internal competitive differences and how they are resolved. This study assumes an elitist power structure of conservative politicians, bureaucrats, and big businessmen, loosely united by a common educational background and a common belief in the private enterprise system but differing in ends and means arising from that value system.

Conflicts of interests among elites, including participants in private economic diplomacy, are resolved through a gradual consensus building process which we shall characterize as "cooperative-competition."[8] It is competition with peaceful coexistence, for Japanese businessmen prefer not to beat the competition to the extent of producing a winner and a loser as in boxing.[9] They are more interested in fighting for a larger piece of the action than for a final decision. The government's role is like a referee who encourages proper balance among competitors, except that the analogy breaks down

---

*An American delegate to the 1969 meeting of the Pacific Basin Economic Council (Chapter 5) remarked: "The Japanese always come prepared with an agreed position; we don't even have a position."

3

since the government and groups that comprise it are themselves
competitors. The system allows the off-the-record expression of
all views held by parties considered to have a legitimate stake in the
issue, but it favors those interests that successfully identify themselves with larger interests, ultimately those of the state.[10] The
competition takes place among politicians, bureaucrats, and businessmen, through formal and informal channels, under clearly understood
rules of behavior. Based on this conceptual approach we can identify
several specific characteristics which apply to Japanese private
economic diplomacy.

First, within the close (though not always harmonious) working
relationship between business and government in Japan, interaction
takes place within a centrally located economic power structure with
easy internal communication, more like that of Great Britain than the
United States,[11] with preconsultation on policy decisions as one of
the ground rules.

Another Japanese characteristic is the degree to which they
have organized the participation of businessmen in diplomacy as a
continuing part-time activity. While American businessmen and
academics are more free to shuffle in and out of the administration,
diplomacy by businessmen in the United States and Western Europe
is sporadic. Germany is comparable to Japan in many ways but
German businessmen were slow to become involved in foreign policy
after the war, except as specialists appointed by the Foreign Ministry
for specific negotiations.[12] As of 1957, at least, there were many
instances of career transfers from business to the Foreign Office
and vice versa, but no organized part-time involvement of businessmen. The Japanese, on the other hand, have developed an elaborate
structure of standing committees, liaison and publication channels,
and even special terminology, that is, private economic diplomacy.
Since the mid-1960s, participation by businessmen in Japanese diplomacy has been considered a constant rather than an intermittant
phenomenon.

While it goes without saying that corporate profits are important
as a motivating factor, equally important is the Japanese characteristic of disassociating economic from commercial activities. The
distinction is easier to maintain in theory than in practice, but it
means that those missions or joint committees which are labeled as
economic should aim for the primary objective of a favorable international environment, leaving the more friction-producing activities
of bargaining and selling to commercial efforts, normally conducted
at another time by less senior, more specialized businessmen. The
Japanese economic mission thus contrasts sharply with the British
statement announcing twenty-five trade missions that were to be sent
to Asia in late 1968: "These are not those pompous missions we used

to send out before—they are real selling missions."[13] This is not to
imply that Great Britain or other countries do not utilize broad purpose
missions. In Britain such missions are sponsored by the Confederation of British Industries (CBI). One CBI mission to the United
States inquired into Japanese exports as a factor in American protectionism.[14] The Japanese approach is to use both economic and
real selling (commercial) approaches extensively but to keep the two
separate and to stress the economic, that is, a general favorable
climate as prerequisite to expanding trade and investment. To understand why this is so we need to briefly trace the historical development of Japanese private economic diplomacy which was influenced
by circumstances of the prewar and Occupation periods.

THE HISTORICAL CONTEXT

Prewar precedents for business involvement in missions abroad
and international meetings occurred as occasional delegations sent
by large industrial combines, or zaibatsu,* which were entirely commercial. They were conceived not as economic missions but as study
teams for the twin purposes of training personnel and expanding
business directly. The only case known to involve top business leaders
was a business sponsored mission that visited the United States,
England, and parts of Europe from October 1921 to May 1922.[15] The
group was led by Baron Takuma Dan of Mitsui Holding Company and
also included Ginjiro Fujiwara of Oji Seishi who was one of the few
business leaders to accept a cabinet post in the prewar period. The
absence of a diplomatic function was due in part to a general failure
by business leaders to identify with interests broader than their own

---

*The term "zaibatsu" is no longer relevant in its prewar meaning
of a group of large Japanese companies under the control of a single
holding company, family owned and controlled. The prewar zaibatsu
groups, purged during the Occupation, are now reorganized loosely
around a bank and trading company rather than family ownership
through holding companies. The more inclusive term "industrial
group," or keiretsu, is becoming the preferred term, specifically,
Mitsubishi group, and so forth. Zaibatsu is retained here to indicate
the three major surviving prewar groups in their reorganized form:
Mitsubishi, Mitsui, and Sumitomo. For a comparison of prewar and
postwar zaibatsu, see Kazuo Noda, Zaibatsu [Financial combines]
(Tokyo: Chuokoransha, 1967). For an analysis of keiretsu, see
Eleanor M. Hadley, Antitrust in Japan (Princeton: Princeton University Press, 1970).

short-term profits. As a corollary to this, businessmen were hard pressed to reconcile profit interests with the ideal of service to the nation.

Marshall's study of Japanese businessmen from the beginning of the Meiji period (1868) to World War II described their awkward attempts to justify private enterprise not by the profit motive, but by the businessman's desire to serve the nation in the tradition of shishi, loyalist samurai of the Meiji Restoration.[16] This collectivist orientation left little room for the philosophy of economic individualism that characterized capitalism in the West. It made justification of private profit more difficult and made the business elite increasingly vulnerable to attack from the socialist left and the ultranationalist right.

During the rise of political parties in the 1920s business sought to protect its interests by identifying with the parties, including financial support to party leaders, but the concern of the business community in politics was confined to serving its own immediate economic ends.[17] Then in the 1930s when the military became a dominating force in government, the relationship between Japanese business and government changed from "the pleasant symbiosis of the 1920's," centering on political parties, to mutual hostility, centering on the military. Mitsui and other industrial groups tried to disassociate themselves from politics to avoid becoming indebted to or identified with government officials. Mitsubishi adopted an explicit policy of nonintervention in politics, putting emphasis instead on its slogan for building national strength through company strength.[18] A few business leaders did manage to participate in government by accepting cabinet offices, and they may have been responsible in large part for preserving the strength of the business community vis-a-vis the bureaucracy and the military until business could regroup after the war.[19] Nevertheless, this uneasy, insecure, and self-seeking relationship between elites provided no basis for the early development of private economic diplomacy.

The postwar Japanese businessman has relatively more security and less inhibitions about espousing the profit motive and the private enterprise system. He was encouraged further in this direction in the latter half of the Occupation by official decisions to depurge business leaders and to shift Occupation policy toward a stronger Japanese economy against the Communist thrust through Korea.[20] He still had to defend himself against being squeezed between public charges of excess profits at the expense of the nation, on the one hand, and government regulation in the name of the national interest, on the other. He quickly developed a new business rhetoric which called for businessmen to go beyond the profit motive to accept social responsibility for Japanese society.* The business community as a whole did not show much zeal in embracing social responsibility,[21] but we are not concerned here with measuring the gap between rhetoric and realization, nor with the rhetoric itself except for what it tells us about the operational interests underlying our subject. Historically, one of these interests has been to give the businessman, his company, and the business community a more favorable public record.

The record of private economic diplomacy in postwar Japan may be said to have begun before the resumption of its professional diplomacy, when Occupation policy prohibited Japanese diplomats being stationed abroad. Near the end of the Occupation, in May 1951, Prime Minister Yoshida asked Katsumi Yamagata, president of Yamashita Shinnihon Steamship, to visit Europe and the United States as a private citizen to seek Allied consent for reconstruction of the Japanese maritime industry. Preliminary negotiations for a general peace treaty had been encountering a hard line among business and government leaders of some of the Allied powers who were fearful that Japanese industries, such as spinning and shipping, might again pose a military threat. Britain, for example, had wanted to insert clauses in the peace treaty that would limit Japanese shipbuilding.[22]

To allay Allied fears, Yamagata visted parliamentarians and cabinet members in Britain, France, and other European countries. In the United States he talked with John Foster Dulles, then Ambassador at Large under Secretary of State Acheson. Dulles in turn introduced him to members of the Senate Foreign Relations Committee. Yamagata's mission was not in vain: Restrictive clauses were not inserted in the Japanese Peace Treaty which went into effect in April 1952 when the Occupation ended.

Scattered missions were sent abroad after 1952 but these were of a technical or commercial nature, that is, they were conducted for educational or business purposes with no assigned responsibility to present Japan's position on specific issues. The shift to more of a diplomatic emphasis gradually became discernible in the top management study teams which were sent abroad by the Japan Productivity Center beginning in 1955.[23] These groups of executives and scholars are classified as technical missions because they were designed to acquaint participants with new management techniques,

---

*Endorsements of the assumption of social responsibility by businessmen can be found in policy statements of all major Japanese business associations, but the idea was first presented by Keizai Doyukai and is associated with that business association. See, for example, the outline of basic policies in Keizai Doyu, October 25, 1965, p. 8.

but over the series of seven teams ending in 1962, participants gradually began to speak out more on economic policy and issues. Thus they were basic to the growth of the economic mission.

A systematic pattern of private economic diplomacy began to emerge in 1956, the starting point for our study. By that year Japan had recovered economically from the war, gross national product equalled $27 billion,[24] and her leaders felt the necessity to take new diplomatic initiatives, some of which we shall follow through 1968. Although selected pre-1956 and post-1968 developments are mentioned where considered germane to the general argument, the data and analysis refer to the 1956-68 period, unless otherwise noted.

In 1961 the Japanese business community invited to Japan Sir Norman Kipping, the director-general of the Federation of British Industries (renamed Confederation of British Industries in August 1965). The initiative for the visit came from Japan's Ambassador Ohno in London, but the presentation of the invitation and subsequent arrangements in Japan were made by Keidanren. At the conclusion of his two-week visit Sir Norman wrote a favorable report, "A Look at Japan,"[25] which was influential in correcting British misconceptions about Japanese cheap labor and exports. According to Ambassador Ohno, it also contributed directly to Britain's decision to conclude a treaty of commerce and navigation with Japan, and coincidentally, to further Japanese interest in the involvement of businessmen in diplomacy.[26]

Finally, this interest took definitive shape in the 1964 government sponsored mission to the United States, led by Yoshizane Iwasa, then president of Fuji Bank, which has served as a model for many subsequent missions.[27] It set a precedent for high standards in selecting members of economc missions on the assumption that the success of an economic mission depended on the caliber of its members. Iwasa's choice of business leaders set the pattern for future missions. Earlier missions had included senior businessmen, but not of such uniformly high caliber and not with policy positions to convey and policy-relevant information to gather. Nor was it coincidental that three mission members—Iwasa, Shigeo Nagano, and the late Masao Anzai—went on to become three of the most active leaders on missions, joint committee, and conferences. They reappear later on the Takasugi mission where Iwasa again had a hand in the selection process.

The primary purpose of the Iwasa mission was to correct American misconceptions about Japan. In major cities throughout the United States Doyukai leader Iwasa and seven business leaders met with high government officials and with leading American businessmen at conferences arranged by The Committee for Economic Development (CED), Doyukai's counterpart organization in the United States.

These talks and formal speeches were aimed at destroying old myths such as the cheap quality of Japanese goods. Iwasa's speeches repeatedly emphasized such points as: (1) Japan is the fifth (third in 1974) ranking industrial power in the world; (2) it has the world's highest sustained growth rate; (3) U.S.-Japanese trade shows an annual advantage to the United States of up to a billion dollars (since 1965 in Japan's favor); (4) Japan is America's second best customer after Canada; and (5) the United States tends to take Japan for granted as an "automatic ally."[28] Iwasa tailored his speeches at each meeting to include regional facts and figures on existing and potential U.S.-Japanese trade applicable to the particular city or area in which he was speaking, always underlining the local benefits of the U.S.-Japan economic partnership.

One of the information-gathering objectives was to listen to a broader cross section of American business than previously, including gathering possible American reactions if Japan were to increase trade with the People's Republic of China.[29] As it has turned out, increases in Sino-Japanese trade, until recently, have been limited by political pressures from Peking, but the shock to the Japanese of the announcement of President Nixon's 1972 visit to Peking illustrates the importance of the information-gathering objective for Japan.

The Iwasa mission will be remembered, not so much for gathering information or for correcting misconceptions held by Americans, but as a model for private economic diplomacy to follow. It spawned new organizations and new regional approaches to the United States' Pacific Coast, Midwest, and South. It had anticipated and confirmed much untapped interest toward Japan in these subregions which had been neglected in the past in favor of New York and Washington. Iwasa himself continued to take a leadership role in missions, joint economic committees, and international businessmen's conferences which are the subjects of subsequent chapters. The events outlined thus far represent only the historical highlights of private economic diplomacy's development into the extensively used instrument it is today.

Other instruments are used equally extensively toward the overall objective of an improved economic climate. Commercial and technical missions, invitational diplomacy such as the Kipping visit, the use of registered lobbyists and economic public relations consultants, international labor conferences, and many other seemingly unrelated activities all make their respective contributions. While retaining the perspective of private economic diplomacy as a portion of this spectrum of activities, we have drawn the topic's boundary lines at its four major forms which we shall examine from the point of view of group and individual interests underlying Japan's drive for economic strength.

NOTES

1. According to a Western journalist, the derogatory phrase "economic animal" was first used several years ago by a former Pakistani foreign minister who intended it to mean that Japan was more interested in economics than in politics. The phrase has persisted, much to Japan's discomfort, more so since the Japanese word for animal (dobutsu) refers only to nonhumans. See Gregory Clark, "The Fragile Face of Force," Far Eastern Economic Review, November 28, 1970, p. 63.

2. Lawrence Olson, Japan in Postwar Asia (New York: Praeger, 1970), pp. 4-6, 72, 194, 219, passim. Olson takes the position that most Japanese government and private representatives had been seeking only profits, at least until the mid-1960s. This study will take a pluralist position and will stress "nonprofit" motives that support profitable trade but that may be considered supracommercial.

3. An important example of the economic mission was the 1964 Iwasa mission to the United States. See "1964 nen ho-Bei keizai shisetsudan hokokusho" [Report of the 1964 economic mission to the United States] (Tokyo: 1964 nen ho-Bei keizai shisetsudan, October 1964), or a shorter English version of the same title published informally by the mission.

4. Our conceptual framework here is drawn from William W. Lockwood: "Seen in this light, both business and the Liberal-Democratic Party, and the top civil service as well, are a network of elitist elements, bargaining vigorously within a framework of consensus on Japan's basic institutions." "Japan's New Capitalism," in The State and Economic Enterprise in Japan, ed. Lockwood (Princeton: Princeton University Press, 1965), p. 516.

5. One American banker put it bluntly: "The only thing really different about the Japanese is that they work harder than the rest of us." Interview with Donald R. Marsh, Vice-President, Morgan Guaranty Trust Company, November 16, 1972. Mr. Marsh spent six years in Japan.

6. Boston Consulting Group, Business Strategies for Japan, ed. James C. Abegglen (Tokyo: Sophia University and Encyclopedia Britannica, 1970).

7. C. Wright Mills, The Power Elite (New York: Oxford University Press, 1956). The "power elite" titles of Hayashi's "Nihon no pawa erito" and Yukio Suzuki's Gendai Nihon no kenryoku erito are straight from Mills. See also works by Noguchi, Mannari, Sakaguchi, Watanuki, and for a particularly pessimistic view, the article by Shigeo Misawa. He warns of a gradual trend toward unification, a "mutual permeation" (sogo shinto), of Japan's ruling elites. "Seisaku kettei katei no gaikan" [Outline of the policy-decision

making process], in Gendai Nihon no seito to kanryo, ed. Nihon Seiji Gakkai (Tokyo: Iwanami Shoten, 1967), p. 19.

8. This phrase was taken from kyochoteki kyoso (cooperative competition) used to characterize Japanese economic mores in Hisao Kanamori, "Ichi oku jin' no keizai energi." [The economic drive of a hundred million people], Ekonomisuto, June 1, 1971, p. 50. See also "Competition but also Cooperation," Japan Economic Journal, June 1, 1971, p. 11, and Derek Davis, "The Challenge of Japan," Far Eastern Economic Review, January 2, 1971, p. 20, and speeches of Kazutaka Kikawada, Chairman of the business association Keizai Doyukai.

9. Adapted from Hidetoshi Kato, "Symposium '71 Japan" (Advertisement), Fortune, August 1971, p. 44.

10. Warren M. Tsuneishi, Japanese Political Style (New York: Harper & Row, 1966), p. 18. Tsuneishi lists holism as one of five Japanese attitudes that bear on politics. He found that questions regarding the relative importance of the individual as opposed to the nation elicited a substantial willingness to subordinate individual wishes to the needs of the higher group.

11. Marshall E. Dimock, The Japanese Technocracy: Management and Government in Japan (New York: Walker/Weatherhill, 1968), p. 98. See also Warren M. Tsuneishi, op. cit., p. 164. Tsuneishi rejects the term "pressure group" for Japanese business associations because the term implies groups which are external to government. Instead, "The government and the trade associations in particular constitute, in a sense, mutual interest groups with the point of contact lying primarily in the executive bureaucracy rather than in the legislature." On the basis of this analysis we shall focus on relevant ministries within the bureaucracy and shall not deal separately with the relationship between the business community and the Diet.

12. Samuel L. Wahrhaftig, "The Development of German Foreign Policy Institutions," in West German Leadership and Foreign Policy, ed. Hans Speier and W. Phillips Davison (Evanston, Ill.: Row, Peterson, 1957), pp. 31-32. There is no mention of an organized involvement of German businessmen in diplomacy, either in this article or an accompanying article, "The Politics of German Business," by Gabriel A. Almond, pp. 195-241.

13. Michael Montagne, Chairman of the Asian Committee of the British National Export Council, as quoted in Japan Times, October 13, 1968, p. 10.

14. Far Eastern Economic Review, March 27, 1971, p. 50.

15. Tokutaro Sakai, ed., Ei Bei homon jitsugyodan shi [Record of the industrial team to visit England and the United States] (Tokyo: Nihon Kogyo Kurabunai Juitchinenkai, 1926). The only known extant copy is available at the library of Keidanren in Tokyo.

16. Byron K. Marshall, Capitalism and Nationalism in Prewar Japan (Stanford, California: Stanford University Press, 1967), pp. 3, 47, 92, 114, passim.

17. Arthur E. Tiedemann, "Big Business and Politics in Prewar Japan," in Dilemmas of Growth in Prewar Japan, ed. James W. Morley (Princeton: Princeton University Press, 1971), pp. 285-86.

18. Yukio Suzuki, Gendai Nihon no kenryoku erito [The power elite in modern Japan] (Tokyo: Bansho Shobo, 1967), pp. 142-51.

19. Tiedemann, op. cit., p. 315. He lists the most prominent businessmen who took Cabinet office: Seihin Ikeda (Mitsui), Ichizo Kobayashi (Mitsui), Ginjiro Fujiwara (Oji Seishi), Shozo Murata (OSK), and Masatsune Ogura (Sumitomo).

20. Robert E. Ward, "The Legacy of the Occupation," in The United States and Japan, ed. Herbert Passin (Englewood Cliffs, N.J.: Prentice-Hall, 1966), pp. 31-56.

21. Japan Economic Journal, June 4, 1968, p. 20 (editorial), and Suzuki, op. cit., p. 125.

22. Sato et al., op. cit., p. 4.

23. M. Y. Yoshino, Japan's Managerial System (Cambridge, Mass.: M.I.T. Press, 1968), p. 103. The Japan Productivity Center (Nihon Seisansei Honbu) was organized in March 1955 with support and participation from business, labor, and academic circles. It sponsors or cosponsors survey teams abroad, brings technicians to Japan for training, and has an active research and publishing program, all toward its goal of increasing labor and management productivity.

24. Economic Planning Agency, Kaitei kokumin shotoku tokei [Revised report on national income statistics] (Tokyo: Ministry of Finance, 1969), p. 60.

25. London: Federation of British Industries, 1961.

26. Sato et al., op. cit., p. 32. The Kipping visit is an example of invitational diplomacy in which government suggests that business extend an invitation. It frequently works in reverse as well. In one instance, Nissan Motors suggested that the Japanese Foreign Ministry invite the Mexican Minister of Trade and Commerce. In such a case it would not be appropriate for Nissan to extend the invitation, but when foreign officials do make such visits the Japanese business community invariably hosts them at receptions and group or private meetings. Thus invitational diplomacy has a definite role as a form of private economic diplomacy, but for the purpose of narrowing our scope we shall not consider it here. We are more concerned with Japanese businessmen in the role of traveling diplomat or working with their counterparts in committees and conferences.

27. "1964 nen ho Bei keizai shisetsudan hokokusho" [Report of the 1964 economic mission to the United States], hereafter cited as Iwasa report (Tokyo: 1964 nen ho Bei keizai shisetsudan, October 1964).

Iwasa selected the presidents of Fuji Iron and Steel, Toyo Rayon, Kawasaki Dockyard, Hitachi Ltd., Nisshin Spinning, Showa Denko (chemical), and Nippon Seiko (bearings). All these men are business leaders. In addition, Iwasa included a labor leader, a journalist, and a professor of economics.

28. "Report of the 1964 Japanese Economic Mission to the United States," published and distributed by the Mission, p. 37. See also "A Straight-from-the-Shoulder Japanese Reminder," Fortune, May 1964, p. 110.

29. Yuichiro Noguchi, "Economic Nationalism," Journal of Social and Political Ideas in Japan 4 (August 1966), p. 96.

2

This chapter will analyze the major participants in private economic diplomacy—ministries, business associations, companies, and individuals—in terms of their overall interest and perhaps more important, their separate interests. The extent to which their underlying interests are mutually reinforcing or conflicting is fundamental to understanding the nature and efficacy of our subject. Where interests conflict we can gain some understanding of the process by which they are resolved in the course of private economic diplomacy.

The overall interest of establishing and maintaining an international climate favorable to Japanese trade and investment was set forth in the previous chapter. This is one of those goals that is never permanently achieved; it pushes out in front of you with each new economic advance. In the decade of the 1960s the Japanese achieved economic strength comparable to that of the advanced Western states,[1] particularly the United States. They accomplished this through the development of heavy industry, postponement of social capital spending, increased exports, and willingness to trade with any country short of jeopardizing political and military ties with the West. In so doing Japan created friction with her trading partners in direct proportion to her economic success. This in turn increased the burden on private economic diplomacy to reestablish a favorable climate—the overall interest—which we shall now break down into its components of participant interests in order to answer the question, favorable to whom and for what?

MINISTRY OF FOREIGN AFFAIRS

The Foreign Ministry has the most at stake in private economic diplomacy because it holds overall responsibility for Japan's foreign

14

relations. This includes planning and administration of foreign policy, conducting diplomatic negotiations, concluding treaties, and carrying out basic research on foreign countries. The Foreign Ministry's interest differs from that of other ministries more by its comprehensiveness than by its intensity. Although the Foreign Ministry has an overall interest, other ministries can be just as interested, especially the Ministry of International Trade and Industry where specific industries or products are concerned.

Throughout 1956-68 Japan identified its overall interest with high economic growth rates, including exports, but since the Foreign Ministry's main interest lies in maintaining good relations—not in trade per se—profitable trade at the expense of good bilateral relations would not be in the Ministry's interest. The Ministry sought a favorable climate through diplomacy in a low key, particularly under Premier Hayato Ikeda (1960-64). Private economic diplomacy was used in a similar manner by attempting to keep the economic and the commercial separate and in balance. Businessmen who were capable of operating in this way could be helpful to the Foreign Ministry, especially where government to government relations were difficult, as in Korea and the Soviet Union.

Help from the business community was also important at home because the Foreign Ministry's strength lies primarily abroad in its many embassies and consulates. Its total staff as of 1963 consisted of only 2,517 employees, compared to 15,449 for MITI and a staggering 86,204 for the Finance Ministry.[2] Moreover, the Foreign Ministry is comparatively weak in personal ties to the business community. It does not participate in the Japanese custom of voluntary retirement at age fifty-five which permits officials thereafter to accept business excutive positions, head interest groups, or enter elective politics— all sources of outside support for the ministries.[3] By utilizing businessmen abroad the Foreign Ministry gained the domestic allies it would not otherwise have to the same extent as other ministries. The Ministry discovered, for example, that sending businessmen observers to international conferences (for example, the U.N. Conference on Coffee) served two purposes: (1) observers added expertise on commercial aspects of a problem; (2) they relayed to domestic business circles the complexities of the problem and what support the Foreign Ministry needs to cope with it. The Ministry can thereby recruit allies to present its point of view to other ministries or to the public.[4]

Of course private economic diplomacy is just one channel by which the Foreign Ministry communicates with business leaders. It is used internationally along with domestic channels such as the Friday Society (Kinyokai), so named because it originally met on the first Friday of each month. The Society was established for informal liaison between the Foreign Ministry and leaders of the business association Keizai Doyukai.[5] Foreign Ministry members include a Vice-Minister, and Doyukai is represented by its chairman, Kazutaka Kikawada, and other business leaders. Such meetings are designed for a free exchange of views on foreign policy issues. Unlike a formal conference, no official record is kept and the discussions are not made available to the public. We shall not attempt to gauge the importance of the Friday Society and other informal policy discussion groups except to observe that such groups are always present, operative, and separate from formal structures.

In terms of formal structure, through 1968 official responsibility for private economic diplomacy within the Foreign Ministry lay with the Economic Affairs Bureau (Keizai Kyoku). The Economic Cooperation Bureau might also become involved when the planned diplomacy included developing countries. Strictly political matters were the responsibility of regional bureaus, for example, North America Bureau, American Section, but the jurisdiction of the Economic Affairs Bureau covered a wide range of issues, given the priority for economics in Japan's foreign policy of 1956-68. Within the Economics Bureau, the Office of General Affairs (Somusanjikanshitsu) drew up the mission's budget and coordinated plans made for each mission by geographic divisions of the Bureau.

After 1968, bilateral economic and political affairs were combined into four regional bureaus: Asian Affairs, American Affairs, European and Oceanic Affairs, and Middle Eastern and African Affairs. These bureaus took over responsibility for private economic diplomacy, leaving multilateral matters and overall coordination to the Economic Affairs and Economic Cooperation Bureaus. The purpose of the change, according to a Ministry spokesman, was "to integrate political and economic operations which have been conducted separately so far."[6] This change was enacted just at the end of our period of study, but as a structural change it may have marked the beginning of a gradual movement away from the economics first foreign policy of the postwar period.

Both the old and the new Foreign Ministry structural arrangements for private economic diplomacy differ from that of the Ministry of International Trade and Industry, which is organized primarily by major and minor industries, and the Finance Ministry, which is organized by functional areas.[7] In each ministry offices that hold responsibility for a particular project would meet, according to need, on two levels. The administrative level (gyoseijo) is sufficient to handle most problems between the ministries. The department head (bucho) is the senior man at this level. If a problem involves basic policy, or if it cannot be solved at the administrative level, it goes up to the political level (seijijo) to be negotiated by the ministries' bureau chiefs, vice-ministers, or ministers.[8]

The distinction between administrative and political levels is not entirely accurate because at all levels the ministries must take into account each other's policy positions and those of business whose influence on a given issue will depend on the degree of unanimity and involvement by business circles.[9] Business views may be represented by businessmen or business association staff members at a level equal to their ministry counterparts (in descending order: bureau, department, division), or indirectly by the Ministry of International Trade and Industry.

MINISTRY OF INTERNATIONAL TRADE AND INDUSTRY (MITI)

MITI can be said to pursue three major interests. First, it attempts to guide business on behalf of the Japanese government. It does this through formal and informal regulation of Japanese and foreign companies. In order to strengthen Japanese industries against foreign incursions, MITI advocates changing corporate units to larger internationally competitive entities subject to government regulation.

Second, MITI attempts to ascertain the views of the Japanese business community and to aggregate them into a consensus for policy purposes. In this capacity MITI uses private economic diplomacy to bring together the many diverse opinions of the Japanese business community by using missions and the like as a medium for communication, a kind of opinion survey.[10]

Third, MITI attempts to represent business views on behalf of the business community. This often means representing business at meetings with the Foreign Ministry.[11] It may also mean providing a platform for Japanese business views abroad through private economic diplomacy. MITI sends businessmen on three types of missions: the industrial economic mission, the private negotiation mission, and the primary products survey.[12]

The industrial economic mission was sent to a country just prior to bilateral government trade negotiations. Businessmen met their counterparts and government officials at private talks in the host country to prepare the way for the official talks which followed. For instance, five or six businessmen with perhaps a MITI observer might make up a MITI industrial economic mission, to the United States steel industry to seek more liberal steel import quotas. Such missions were budgeted at three per year.

The private negotiation mission was timed concurrently with government negotiations, normally for the purpose of removing discriminatory trade restrictions against Japanese goods. According to MITI such missions had been highly successful but they always focused on a specific product or industry, primarily in Europe because of conservative postwar trade policies there. Four teams per year were budgeted for this type of mission.

The primary products survey was designed to further economic cooperation and trade expansion with developing countries. It was the only type in which the government paid expenses of all members of the mission. In other cases the government paid for the mission leader while other members' expenses had to be paid by their respective companies.

These three types of MITI mission all involve businessmen, but their purpose is limited to narrow, specific industries or products, not the broad favorable climate objective of our definition. MITI occasionally sends an individual as an observer on broader gauge missions, and must be consulted frequently, depending on the sponsor and purpose.

Liaison with the Foreign Ministry concerning one of its economic missions was the responsibility of MITI's International Trade Policy Division (Tsusho Seisakka) of the International Trade Bureau (Tsusho Kyoku) in conjunction with the Bureau's three (four by 1974) geographic divisions. Liaison with business associations for a business sponsored mission was the responsibility of the Second Division (Kigyo Nika) of the Industrial Policy Bureau (Kigyo Kyoku). Here business explained how it intended to represent Japanese industrial policies on a particular mission, joint economic committee meeting, or international conference. In the case of MITI's own missions, the Trade and Development Division of the Trade and Development Bureau (Boeki Shinko Kyoku) was in charge of budgeting and planning since the objective was trade promotion not the general economic climate.

MITI's spokesman made it clear that economic missions were the primary responsibility of the Foreign Ministry. On the other hand, if MITI feels it has a legitimate interest it may compete with the Foreign Ministry for jurisdiction. When in the fall of 1972 it was decided to send the first government economic mission to the People's Republic of China, MITI sought to be its sponsor but lost out to the Foreign Ministry which has primary jurisdiction as long as the main objective is the establishment or improvement of diplomatic relations.[13] This was another application of the economic/commercial distinction which, in oversimplified terms, resolves jurisdictional disputes by identifying the Foreign Ministry with economic interests and MITI with commercial interests.

The distinction is not always as easy to apply as it is to make, since MITI does have broad responsibilities. MITI drafts the basic legislation that controls foreign trade. It administers such controls through licensing, regulation of patent agreements, administration of the Import-Export Law, and supervision of economic and trade agreements.

In pursuing these interests in the 1960s MITI leaders came to be known as "new structure bureaucrats"[14] because of MITI's policy line which was close to what some business circles were saying yet reflected MITI's own interests. The new structure bureaucrats wanted to reorganize Japanese industry by weakening the Anti-Monopoly Law to encourage mergers and cartels under government (MITI) regulation. In cooperation with business, MITI bureaus would take measures to concentrate and specialize production, force mergers where necessary, rationalize subcontracting among small firms, standardize parts and models, and expand markets by installment selling and export credits. It also would have restructured the banking system by having government rather than commercial banks finance private equipment investment. These policy proposals naturally brought MITI into conflict at some points with other ministries and with business itself, depending on the particular business opinion group or business association.

KEIDANREN (JAPAN FEDERATION OF ECONOMIC ORGANIZATIONS)

As the most prestigious of the business associations and the leading nongovernment sponsor of private economic diplomacy, Keidanren attempts to perform three functions:[15] (1) adjust differing interests of industries and corporations on behalf of the business community as a whole; (2) formulate and present policy recommendations to the government; and (3) promote international exchange.[16]

It seeks to adjust or harmonize business interests through an elaborate organizational structure which in 1971 comprised 700 firms, a few individual members, and 105 regional and trade federations. The trade federations do not participate in private economic diplomacy since they only represent companies within a single industry or group of industries. For example, the Electronic Industries Association of Japan or the Japan Cotton Textile Exporters' Association have sufficient finances and staff to represent their interests politically, and they often send commercial missions abroad, but they participate in economic missions through Keidanren. In other words, organizational sponsorship depends on the economic/commercial distinction.

Much of the adjustment of business interests is done in connection with Keidanren's second function, formulating and presenting policy recommendations to government, which are drafted and debated in standing committees. By 1968 the number of these Keidanren committees had grown to twenty-six, almost all of which are concerned with economic problems.[17] The power to adopt a policy position, or return it to committee for further study, lies with the president and eight vice-presidents (one seat vacant), although major decisions must be approved formally by a vote of the Board of Directors and the General Assembly. Once approved, a position paper is transmitted to the appropriate government agency and announced to the press. Of course, before it reaches this stage there will have been preconsultation, probably with ministry division chiefs on up to vice-ministers or minister. Keidanren normally appoints a former foreign service officer to provide full-time liaison capability with the Foreign Ministry.[18]

The content of Keidanren's policy recommendations can be characterized as laissez-faire, mainstream business thinking,[19] and conservative, although pro-trade liberalization relative to certain of Keidanren's company and trade federation members.

In 1968 some members of Keidanren's liberalization committee expressed opinions in favor of early liberalization of foreign investment in the automobile industry. This shocked automobile executives who immediately pressed Keidanren to exclude automobiles from its list of industries recommended for early liberalization.[20] If it were the case that the opinions in favor of early liberalization for automobiles grew out of discussions at a joint economic committee or international businessmen's conference, then private economic diplomacy may serve the purpose not only of presenting Japanese views internationally, but of modifying those views internally according to the interests of the participants. In other words, private economic diplomacy may belong under all three of Keidanren's functions, not merely promoting international exchange.

In the policy dialogue with government, for example, mainstream businessmen seek some form of "effective competition"* under which business would keep its own house in order without government regulation. It is therefore in Keidanren's interest to cooperate with MITI in promoting mergers but to compete with it for authority to regulate business. Keidanren under President Taizo Ishizaka (1956-68) was lukewarm, to say the least, on proposals by MITI's new structure bureaucrats for government-business cooperation.

Keidanren's third function, promoting international exchange, is coordinated by its International Economic Affairs Department.

---

*"Effective competition" (yuko kyoso) is a vague goal sought by Japanese businessmen to replace present day "excessive competition" (kato kyoso), a term often found in the Japanese press referring to too many Japanese companies competing with each other in a given industry. The two terms, of course, mean different things to different people. Presumably effective competition would require industrial reorganization through mergers toward fewer but stronger firms.

Policy questions for a particular delegation are handled by the appropriate standing committee, for example, Internationalization Promotion,
but administrative aspects are the responsibility of International
Economic Affairs, often including assigning a staff member to travel
with a delegation. Preparatory and follow-up phases are also busy.
Delegates must all receive background materials and the formal report afterward must be reviewed, published, and adapted for brief
internal reports and publication in the house organs, Keidanren Geppo
and Keidanren Review. The highly structured way in which Keidanren
promotes international exchange is evidenced by Keidanren's pre-
dominant role as a sponsor of economic missions and joint economic
committees in particular, thus serving her self-interests by reinforcing
Keidanren's status as the principal representative of the Japanese
business community at home and abroad.

NISSHO (JAPAN CHAMBER OF COMMERCE AND INDUSTRY)

As primarily a federation of some 453 local chambers of commerce, Nissho* includes the interests of medium and small business
which, in a dual economy like Japan's, are bound to conflict with the
interests of big business.† Consequently, Nissho has difficulty speaking
with one voice. Moreover, its special members include foreign chambers of commerce in Japan as well as the less surprising regional
federations of chambers of commerce, public enterprises, and national
commercial and industrial associations. Of course this does not mean
that decision-making power is so broadly based. Although policy
decisions are subject to approval at semiannual general assemblies,
executive power lies with a conference of the president, five vice-
presidents, executive and managing directors, and a board.[21]
If it cannot compete with Keidanren to represent the interests
of big business domestically, Nissho can still play a leading role as
an organizational link with international business by capitalizing on

---

*Nihon Shoko Kaigisho, abbreviated Nissho, is the oldest of
the major business associations, having been established in 1922.
After the war it was affiliated with Keidanren but withdrew in 1952
along with the Medium and Light Industry Association.

†Structural change to resolve the dualism between large and
small low productivity business is made more difficult by the fact
that large manufacturers have a paternal relationship with small
specialized manufacturers who provide component parts on subcon-
tract. See Seymour Broadbridge, Industrial Dualism in Japan (Chicago:
Aldine, 1966).

its counterpart organizations at home and abroad. It has a major interest in the maintenance and expansion of its international contacts for its own prestige and the commercial benefits of its members, hence its active sponsorship of economic and commercial missions, committees, and conferences.

The burden of staff support for private economic diplomacy within Nissho falls largely on the Foreign Trade section of the Tokyo Chamber of Commerce whose offices and staff are for all practical purposes indistinguishable from Nissho itself. The staff at this level is capable of research, itinerary planning, speech writing, and other secretariat responsibilities for the president directly or an entire delegation. Secretariat capability is important to the personal interests of a businessman, for to be active as a leader in private economic diplomacy he must have an organizational and staff base from which to operate. Nissho presidents, Tadashi Adachi during the period of our study and more recently Shigeo Nagano, both made maximum use of this staff capability in their frequent overseas activities.

KEIZAI DOYUKAI (JAPAN COMMITTEE FOR ECONOMIC DEVELOPMENT)

As a policy spokesman for the Japanese business community, Keizai Doyukai (or simply Doyukai)22 competes with Keidanren, but in structure and function Doyukai has its own specialty, as do each of the other two business associations that are major sponsors of private economic diplomacy.* Doyukai's specialty is to enlighten the individual businessman and to develop for the business community a broad long-term point of view.

There is a certain identity problem inherent in Doyukai's attempt to speak for the business community on policy matters, since

_____

*The fourth major association is Nihon Keieisha Dantai Remmei (Japan Employers Association), abbreviated Nikkeiren. It was formed after the war to meet the need for a management organization specializing in labor problems. It quickly became involved in a major confrontation with the largest labor union federation. Nikkeiren accepts the concept of the labor-capital struggle and undertakes research and counseling for strike problems along with a public relations campaign through the mass media. The nature of this role makes it a poor vehicle for economic diplomacy. Some of its leaders are active in many ways, but as an organization it limits its role to annually sponsoring three to five regional missions which are always confined to labor-management problems.

historically Doyukai represented an antimainstream minority of younger executives who first organized in 1946 in an atmosphere of shock from defeat in the war. The first gathering consisted of some eighty company directors, managers, and department heads who did not rank with the presidents and board chairman generally associated with Keidanren. Recognizing the need for basic changes for postwar construction, Doyukai made a virtue of its junior status by identifying management with youth and progressive ideas. The central concept was one of "revised capitalism" which required the assumption of social responsibility by management and the structural reform of business under a single policy coordinating body or industrial league which would cooperate with government. These structural reform proposals by Doyukai were quite unlike the laissez-faire approach advocated by Keidanren, but they were not incompatible with the government-business cooperation aspects of proposals by MITI's new structure bureaucrats. Thus one may speak of business ideologies in the plural, but not of a single business ideology. Business ideology, such as it is, has no priesthood or "line." It is created, debated, and revised piecemeal among groups of its own adherents.[23]

By 1968 Doyukai's leaders had become senior and some had taken on leadership roles in Keidanren or other organizations, depending on their perception of their own self-interests. Therefore, one should avoid overdrawing a competitive dividing line between major business associations. It is more accurate to say that membership in the associations overlap and that each association performs a special function for the business community, Doyukai's is the intellectual function; to educate and speak for the individual businessman and his relationship to society.

Doyukai's participation in private economic diplomacy is consistent with its intellectual function, with an emphasis on conferences and study groups designed to produce joint policy statements for publication.[24] Moreover, it is consistent with Doyukai's strong international orientation and program, including sending teachers abroad and other projects in cooperation with counterpart organizations in other countries.

Like its foreign counterparts, Doyukai consists entirely of individual businessmen (985 as of 1971) which makes it structurally unique among the major Japanese business associations.[25] This has several ramifications for Doyukai style in private economic diplomacy. First, it is more personal and less bureaucratic, favoring informal conferences although Doyukai also sponsors missions and joint committees. Although it has a chairman, five vice-chairmen, and standing committees as does Keidanren, it has a more simple staff structure. In fact, staff coordination for the entire 1956-68 period was largely the work of a single individual, Secretary-General Seiichi Yamashita, who acted as the right hand man of successive Doyukai leaders Iwasa and Kikawada. Their record of active leadership held alongside of their climb to the top as business leaders suggest that competition for appointments within private economic diplomacy may be as much a function of individual interests as it is of group interests. But before dealing with the question of individual interests let us consider the Japanese company.

COMPANIES

The business of a company is to make money. Japanese companies are hardly an exception, but it is worthwhile noting the greater emphasis that Japanese companies place on market share as contrasted to the emphasis of Western companies on earnings. The ultimate objective is the same—profits—but there is a certain parallel in private economic diplomacy: The Japanese prefer an active program spread as widely as possible but keeping sales in the background and separate from the objective of a favorable climate. For example, the visit by Shigeo Nagano to the Soviet Union in 1967 for the second meeting of the Japan-Soviet Joint Cooperation Committee provided an opportunity to visit Soviet steel mills. What he saw led later to the commercial purchase by Nagano's company, Fuji Iron and Steel, of a Soviet blast furnace steam cooling high pressure system. The distinction drawn by the Japanese between economic and commercial interests may or may not be artifically drawn for tactical purposes, but it is real in terms of time and energy spent on each by the company executive, normally a board chairman, president, or vice-president.

At the company level business competition is most intense, yet before action on business matters can be taken in any company, many decisions must proceed from the lowest initiating level, that is the section, up through the department, the division, and the managing director. This slow process is followed despite great pressure to increase production, sales, and market share. Fifty-hour work weeks are not uncommon and competition is keen among both individuals and companies on a worldwide basis. No doubt this is one reason for the strictly-for-profit reputation of Japanese companies abroad.

On the other hand, a generous amount of time is devoted by top executives to private economic diplomacy and even to noncommercial visits by foreigners. This is made possible by the delegation of day-to-day decisions to subordinates which, together with the elevation of decision-making responsibility from below, places a heavy burden of responsibility at the managing director level. The president is still involved and ultimately responsible for company decisions but having reached the top management level he has more time for outside activities than has his Western counterpart.* In this context private economic diplomacy can be viewed as compensation for, rather than an extension of, one's service to the company. It provides the internationally inclined executive in particular with a natural outlet for his energies outside the narrow confines of his company and its products.

Even if freed from some of his company responsibilities, the executive needs staff support to fulfill the demands of participation in private economic diplomacy, for example, preparation of position papers. He can do this either by holding a concurrent post (hence full use of staff) with Keidanren, Nissho, or Doyukai, or as is often the case, by utilizing an assistant within the company. This person may be given any one of a large number of vague titles, depending on his other duties, but his job is a traveling secretary for the executive's relations with foreigners. Such an assistant will be young, bright, fluent in English, capable of thinking from an international point of view, and will have served the company in at least one foreign country. He may travel with his boss when appropriate, handle travel arrangements, interpret if necessary (the older the executive the more likely his English is poor), and do a good deal of ghost writing. In short, while they are careful to maintain a low posture at international events, these assistants, along with the professional interpreters, make Japanese private economic diplomacy work as well as it does.†

Despite the assistant's close proximity to top management, his position is not one of power within the company. Just as private economic diplomacy is considered somewhat removed from company interests, the international assistant is considered off to the side in the corporate ladder. To climb to the top the young executive must work long and hard on company business. He has little time for international conferences and such. If he is assigned to an overseas post,

---

*The most ambitious American conference is the International Industrial Conference which is held every four years by Stanford Research Institute and the National Industrial Conference Board. Over 400 executives from all over the world attended the 1969 Conference in San Francisco's Fairmont Hotel, but this type of five-day extravaganza on broad policy problems is a rare expenditure of time for top American executives.

†This study would not have been possible without the cooperation and thoughtful insights of several of these internationally oriented junior executives; Masahisa Segawa of Fuji Bank, Masaya Sasaki of Fuji Steel, Kunio Okabe of Yawata Steel, and K. E. Hiroshima of Marubeni-Iida Trading. Their chief colleague among the professional interpreters was Masami Muramatsu of Simul International.

he frequently regards it as decreasing his chances for promotion because he is farmed out, out of sight of his superiors at the home office. As of 1968, it was still the pattern to value involvement in noncommercial international activities only upon reaching the vice-president level. If so, it raises the question of who does seek involvement and why at that particular time in one's career.

THE INTERNATIONALIST BUSINESS LEADER

Businessmen who play leading roles, whether in economic missions and the like or in influential domestic policy groups, are nearly always drawn from a relatively small circle of men known collectively as zaikai. The individual zaikaijin, translated here as "business leader," is not simply a successful businessman, but a successful businessman who is in a position to influence national economic policy and at the same time can speak from the point of view of business as a whole rather than only of individual enterprises.[26] His prestige and power rest on a combination of three bases: social position, company affiliation, and outside activities.[27]

A business leader's social base is fundamental; it comprises his family background and wealth, his education (particularly the prestige of his college), and his blood ties.[28] The blood ties are often of a complex nature, and Japanese writers go to great pains to compile genealogies, but although these ties can indicate political influence, they constitute only one variable in the social base which will be used here as an analytical concept without any attempt to measure influence.

Of equal importance to social position is the type of industry of one's company.[29] Companies range in social esteem, for example, from the heavy manufacturing and mining industries, which are most prestigious, to the banks, which rank somewhere near the middle, to the mass media, which rank lower; the movie industry is excluded altogether from the zaikai regardless of company size or profits. Exceptions to this analysis of one's company base as a stepping stone to power will be mentioned in the biographical sketches below, but whatever the industry, company membership in a major industrial group, especially a former zaibatsu group, is considered advantageous to one's career. It is also commonly thought that to be respected, a Japanese businessman must work his way up through a single company. This was not borne out by the evidence. The business leaders examined below demonstrated a need for a company base but not necessarily in a single company throughout one's career.

Finally, a business leader must engage in many activities outside his company; he must be active in all kinds of committees and groups such as business associations, study groups, policy advisory bodies, political faction support groups, and informal luncheon and dinner groups. It is not enough that he merely participate; he must assume leadership roles in his activities, especially in major business associations. This "activity base" broadens the business leader's public image, multiplies his contacts, and strengthens his voice within and for the business community. Private economic diplomacy can thus be interpreted as a component of a business leader's activity base which serves the career interests of those who choose to be active in it.

There is enough in common among such men for Japanese writers to refer to an "internationalist faction";[30] we shall characterize them as internationalist business leaders. These men see Japan's economic strength as irrevocably linked with a strong world economy. By working through private economic diplomacy they become conveyors of a global point of view abroad and contributors to the dialogue over economic policy within Japan. A Western journalist characterizes two opposing perspectives in the domestic dialogue: a nationalist faction which thinks in terms of unilateral strength, and "a more internationalist faction which sees the relationship with the United States as basic to Japan's economic progress and security and wishes to see Japan play a greater role, not only vis-a-vis its own region, but in peaceful cooperation and competition with the United States, the Socialist bloc, China and the Pacific Basin."[31] The internationalists are not less "Japanese" than the nationalists; but their style of leadership through private economic diplomacy applies the Japanese preference for personal face-to-face relationships to foreign businessmen and government officials, contacts which they value for national interests, the domestic groups of which they are members, and their own careers. We have chosen for illustration seven internationalist business leaders who were among the most important for the 1956-68 period. They are sketched briefly below in conjunction with Tables 1-3 to show how active participation in private economic diplomacy is in their personal interest because it offers a natural extension to their power and prestige as business leaders.

None of the seven are identified with former zaibatsu (Mitsubishi, Mitsui, or Sumitomo) industrial groups. The first two men listed, Tadashi Adachi of Nissho and Taizo Ishizaka of Keidanren, were known for not favoring any company or industrial group, no doubt a factor in their appointments as heads of business associations. All persons interviewed for this study agreed that much of the power in the business community still resides with former zaibatsu member firms but that appointments are made so as not to show favoritism to any industrial group. Sometimes this means choosing men not from Mitsubishi, Mitsui, and Sumitomo, or at least not closely identified as

TABLE 1

Selected Individual Leaders in Private Economic Diplomacy
(chairmanships held of the events surveyed, 1956–68)

Name, Age, and Office	Total	'56	'57	'58	'59	'60	'61	'62	'63	'64	'65	'66	'67	'68
Adachi, Tadashi (85) Past Pres., Nissho	23		1	1	2		1	1	2	2	2	6	3	2
Ishizaka, Taizo (82) Past Pres., Keidanren	12						1	1			3	2	3	2
Nagano, Shigeo (68) Ch., Nippon Steel	10			1			1				1		3	4
Uemura, Kogoro (74) Pres., Keidanren	9	1		1			1				2	2	2	
Iwasa, Yoshizane (62) Pres., Fuji Bank	8						2	1		1	1	1	1	1
Kikawada, Kazutaka (69) Pres., Tokyo Elec. Power	6								1	1			2	2
Kobayashi, Atura (69) Pres., Arabian Oil	2		1										1	

Note: Tabulated from 167 missions, roving ambassadors, joint committee meetings and conferences for which names of individual leaders were available from the total sample of 176 (Appendix A). If complete data on names were obtained, the above figures would increase but the relative order would remain approximately the same. Ages and offices are as of 1968.

Sources: Official reports (see the Bibliography); Ministry of Foreign Affairs, Waga Gaiko no kinkyo [present state of our foreign relations] (Tokyo: Ministry of Finance, annual); Keidanren Geppo; Keidanren Review; Records of Keizai Doyukai and Keidanren, particularly, "Kaigi haken keizai shisetsudanra hokokusho tenji mokuroku" [Catalog of reports on overseas economic missions and the like] (Tokyo: Keizai Dantai Rengokai, 1971); Japanese and English language newspapers.

TABLE 2

Deliberative Council Activities of Selected Business
Leaders
(selected members and chairmen as of July 1, 1970)

Name	Office	Deliberative Councils
Adachi, Tadashi	Past Pres., Nissho	Ch., Postal Service, and member of 7 others
Ishizaka, Taizo	Past Pres., Keidan-ren	Ch., Central Deliberative Council for National Property
Nagano, Shigeo	Ch., Nippon Steel	Member of 10
Uemura, Kogoro	Pres., Keidanren	Ch., Industrial Structure
Iwasa, Yoshizane	Pres., Fuji Bank	Member of 8
Kikawada, Kazutaka	Pres., Tokyo Elec. Power	Ch., Economic Deliberation
Kobayashi, Ataru	Pres., Arabian Oil	Ch., Financial System Ch., Foreign Investment

Note: These deliberative councils are official policy advisory
bodies to the government. Members are drawn from universities,
journalism, labor, the arts, business and government, in order to
provide the appropriate ministry with a cross section of leadership
opinion.

Source: Mainichi Daily News, January 20, 1971.

such, for example, Adachi and Ishizaka. The many appointments of
these two men as leaders in private economic diplomacy (Table 1)
may have been partially due to the business association posts alone,
but the principle still applies—nonfavoritism in representing the
business community.

The above suggests that private economic diplomacy offers
less recognized leaders an arena in which they can compete to advantage with men from prewar industrial groups who have an edge in
the traditional arena. We shall treat this formulation as a corollary
hypothesis, part of the cluster of interests which we are postulating,
which may or may not apply in each case.

Tadashi Adachi

Tadashi Adachi, who became 85 in 1968, ranks with Taizo Ishizaka as the grand old man of the business community and of private economic diplomacy (see Table 1). Their active leadership is interpreted here as due to their preeminent business association positions rather than as a means to gain even higher status, except perhaps to gain the recognition internationally that they already had domestically.

Adachi's social base includes graduation from the Higher Commercial School in Tokyo (the present Hitotsubashi University) and relatives with executive posts in the petroleum, construction, and paper industries. Adachi himself chose Oji Paper as a company base after an initial seven years with Mitsui Trading. He reached the top as Oji's president in 1942-46 so that by 1956 he was already devoting most of his time to his activity base.

TABLE 3

Regional Specialities of Selected Business Leaders

Name and Office	Specialty	Posts Held
Adachi, Tadashi Past Pres., Nissho	Australia, Korea, Republic of China	Chairman of many committees
Ishizaka, Taizo Past Pres., Keidanren	France, United States, United Kingdom	Ch., joint committees
Nagano, Shigeo Ch., Nippon Steel	Pacific Basin, USSR, India	Pres., PBEC mission, com. ch.
Uemura, Kogoro Pres., Keidanren	NONE: As pres. of Keidanren, Uemura attempts to coordinate business activities in general.	
Iwasa, Yoshizane Pres., Fuji Bank	U.S. West Coast, Southeast Asia	Ch., J-Calif. Assoc., Ch., PICA
Kikawada, Kazutaka Pres., Tokyo Elec. Power	U.S. Midwest, West Germany	Mission, assoc, Ch. Ch., Keizai Doyukai
Kobayashi, Ataru Pres., Arabian Oil	Developing countries	Roving Amb., SE Asia, Latin America

Sources: Interviews and reports of missions, conferences, and joint committees.

30

As head of Nissho, Adachi was a natural choice to lead economic missions and the like, but he also possessed the right personal attributes. He was unusually friendly and outgoing for a Japanese, yet he was careful never to appear overly friendly to any group or individual, an important attribute in the selection process of private economic diplomacy. If a Mitsui man is chosen for one delegation then a Mitsubishi or Sumitomo man should be chosen for the same or following delegation. Despite Adachi's early ties to the Mitsui group, he seems to have earned a reputation for objectivity throughout the business community.

Taizo Ishizaka

Taizo Ishizaka held the presidency of Keidanren from 1956 to 1968, the period of our study and an era in which no one challenged his authority as "prime minister of the business world."[32] His power rested as much on his personal qualities as on his title or connections, although he did have the best of educational credentials, graduation from the law department of Tokyo University.* Believing strongly in free enterprise and the strength of the Japanese economy, he favored a bootstrap approach by the business community, without interference by bureaucrats and politicians. He had earlier mounted his own bootstrap operation at Toshiba where he made his reputation by solving a serious labor dispute and regenerating the company. Toshiba has ties with the Mitsui group but none so close that Ishizaka could be accused of being a Mitsui man. In avoiding obligatory ties to industrial, bureaucratic, or political groups, Ishizaka was able to maintain an objectivity which is essential to his post at Keidanren, and to the selection process of private economic diplomacy.

Ishizaka was also known for his international point of view, especially for his affinity for industrialized Western societies. He had an excellent command of the English language, served as an advisor to Chase Manhattan Bank, and was responsible for the establishment of joint economic committees and conferences with England, France, and the United States. He is said to have disliked similar roles with communist countries which in our data took the form of

---

*According to a 1959 survey, 300 of 900 top management positions in Japanese industry were held by graduates of Tokyo University. Tsuneishi, Japanese Political Style (New York: Harper & Row, 1966), p. 80. For biographies and companies of specific Todai graduates, see Diamondosha, ed., Tokyo Daigaku Shusshin [Graduates of Tokyo University] (Tokyo: Diamondosha, 1967).

an approximate East-West division of labor between Ishizaka and Adachi or others (see Table 3).

Shigeo Nagano

Shigeo Nagano has held more than 300 offices simultaneously.[33] He began, not surprisingly, by graduating from the law department of Tokyo University with a major in politics. His brother Mamoru was elected to the Diet in 1942 and served as the Minister of Transportation in Premier Kishi's third cabinet. Shigeo himself remained within business circles except as an advisor to MITI and one year in 1946 as Deputy Director, Economic Stabilization Board, at the request of his old high school classmate, Hiro Wada. Nagano was a close friend of former Premier Ikeda and as such was labeled by the Japanese press as director of the "Ikeda School" and one of the "Four Emperors" of the business community.

Along the way, Nagano managed to maintain an exhaustive activity schedule (see Tables 1-3), including leadership positions in all four major business associations, from a 1946 originating role in Doyukai to the presidency of Nissho in 1969. Even his leisure time was devoted to achievement, earning him seventh rank in judo and fourth rank in the game of go. As one of the most active business leaders in private economic diplomacy, Nagano proved particularly adept at involving himself in significant trends before their significance became clear. He was a roving ambassador to the Soviet Union in 1958, later personally conveyed to Moscow Japan's approval of establishing the Japan-Soviet Joint Cooperation Committee, and chaired the committee's second session. Nagano was also instrumental in starting the Japan-Australia joint committee and moved from there to the establishment of the Pacific Basin Economic Council on which he served as both Japanese and overall president. One finds in these activities a natural correlation with steel and iron ore interests—Australia, Canada, Siberia, India—for Nagano's company and the Japanese steel industry, yet he has placed these interests and his personal ambitions in the larger context of his ability to act in the interests of the entire business community if not Japan itself.

Kogoro Uemura

Kogoro Uemura gained a desirable social base from his father, a past president of Sapporo Beer, and in his degree from Tokyo University. However, he is noteworthy in our analysis for his apparent lack of a company base. Although he was president of the Japan

32

Broadcasting Company and served as a director for several companies, he is primarily a bureaucrat, going back to his first job in the Ministry of Agriculture and Commerce to the prewar Cabinet Planning Board where he served as deputy director-general. He continued this economic bureaucrat role in 1941 as a director of the Coal Control Committee. After the war he became the vice-chairman of the Economic Federation Committee (Keizai Rengo Iinkai) which amalgamated four existing economic organizations. In 1946 this committee became Keidanren and Uemura its managing director. He became executive vice-president in 1952 and served for sixteen years. With this background, Keidanren itself is Uemura's company base, the important factor being that the organization is of and for business.

The Japanese emphasis on loyalty and length of service must also have been an important factor in Uemura's appointment, for he certainly lacks the leadership qualities of an Ishizaka. Instead, Uemura depends on his ability to listen to all views and bring them gradually to a consensus. This means more of a collective leadership style at Keidanren, evidenced by the change from five vice-president slots under Ishizaka, to eight under Uemura.

Uemura's relationship to private economic diplomacy was and is an active one, although simply one of carrying out the regular responsibilities of his own job. He does have a personal interest, however, in using it to maintain his somewhat insecure leadership position as an individual (see discussion of Kikawada below) together with that of Keidanren as a group through its control and sponsorship of economic missions, and joint economic committees in particular.

Yoshizane Iwasa

Yoshizane Iwasa was 62 in 1968, the youngest of the seven business leaders selected for our sample. He began his career ideally with graduation from the law department of the Tokyo University. His father was a military man but young Iwasa became an Iwasa and a banker by the not uncommon step of younger sons being adopted, in this case by a director of the Industrial Bank of Japan, just before graduation.

The strength of Iwasa's company base is less clear than one might expect from the fact that Fuji Bank became Japan's largest under his management. He had joined its forerunner, Yasuda Bank, upon graduation from Tokyo University but he left the bank for broader experience before and during the war, and is considered a postwar leader, having become vice-president of Fuji Bank in 1957. He became chairman of Doyukai in 1959, and only much later a vice-president of Keidanren. Part of this "newcomer" image arose from the failure

of the Yasuda group to reconstitute itself after the war as did Mitsubishi, Mitsui, and Sumitomo, so the advantage of a company base
in a former zaibatsu industrial group does not apply even though a
Fuji group of independent companies had achieved loose intragroup
cooperation by 1968. Moreover, Iwasa's position as a banker was
no particular advantage to his status as a business leader, at least
in comparison to heavy industry.

Iwasa's prominent leadership role in private economic diplomacy
meshed nicely in timing as an extension of his company base. He
became president of Fuji Bank in 1963, led the mission to the United
States in the following year, and has never let up since. Through 1968
he led eight major delegations (see Table 1). One is tempted to say
that he became a Private Economic Ambassador to the United States
West Coast on the basis of the 1964 mission and subsequent leadership
roles in the Japan-California Association and the Pacific Basin Economic Council. The regional specializations of Table 3, however,
are informal at most and were extrapolated by the author from the
general data.

Kazutaka Kikawada

Kazutaka Kikawada chose to study economics at Tokyo University.
Immediately upon graduation he joined Tokyo Electric Light and stayed
with it through its name change to Tokyo Electric Power where he
became president in 1961. He built on this company base to become
the president of the Federation of Electric Power Companies in 1964.
Politically, he was considered to be closer to former Premier Sato
than any other businessman except perhaps Iwasa or Masao Anzai of
Showa Denko Chemical.[34]
Like Iwasa, Kikawada started his activity base with Doyukai
which nicely suited his individualistic and outspoken personal style
and ideological bent toward a strong, self-regulated "revised capitalism" with emphasis on the assumption of more social responsibility
on the part of the business community. Unlike Iwasa, he chose not
to shift his leadership from Doyukai to Keidanren. He refused a vice-
presidency in Keidanren and kept the chairmanship of Doyukai, since
if he had accepted the Keidanren vice-presidency he would have associated himself with policy positions derived from a rather bureaucratic committee structure, thus limiting his individual initiative.
Instead, in 1966 he became a principal organizer of the informal but
prestigious business group, the Industrial Problems Research Society.[35]
Kikawada's interests are difficult to dissect; certainly an electric power company stands to gain little through private economic

diplomacy. His enthusiasm for international affairs appears to be more personal and ideological. He spoke warmly of strengthening ties of worldwide private enterprise, particularly with Germany and the United States,[36] which he was able to achieve through Doyukai's counterpart organizations. He also heads Japanese members of the Japan-Midwest Association (Chapter 6), and is a good friend of Senator Hubert Humphrey. Yet impressive as his activity base is, including Doyukai, Sanken, and the Economic Deliberation Council,[37] it remains to be seen whether his social and company bases, strong ideological views, and maverick style will earn him the support of key industrial groups necessary for any further elevation of his position.

Ataru Kobayashi

Ataru Kobayashi is perhaps the most interesting business leader of all, more for what he did not do, than for what he did. He has at times been more influential than other business leaders, makes far more money,[38] yet has very few of the right "credentials." He is a college dropout, leaving Weseda University after two years. He was adopted into the Kobayashi family but had almost no influential relatives except Naotsugu Nabeshima, a member of the House of Councillors. Even more significant, Kobayashi changed companies and industries, leaving him with a weak company base for much of his career. He started out with Fukoku Life Insurance, switched at the presidency level to Tokyo Express Railroad, switched again as president of the Japan Development Bank (1951-57) under Premier Yoshida, and switched again later to director, then president, of Arabian Oil Company.

Despite an unusual career pattern, and an activity base that shows only two isolated instances of leadership in private economic diplomacy (see Table 1), Kobayashi is an example of flexible adaptation, rather than an exception to the traditional bases of power. He compensated for a weak social base by analytical brilliance in business and politics while keeping away from the spotlight. He compensated for a weak company base by developing specialities in labor problems and international development which led to a permanent director post in Nikkeiren and the presidency of the Overseas Technical Cooperation Agency. These posts, in conjunction with advising government officials (see Table 2), amounted to a strong activity base which had little need for private economic diplomacy, particularly since its high visibility did not suit Kobayashi's distaste for publicity. He is even said to dislike travel because he prefers Japanese food, but all of this notwithstanding, Kobayashi has to be ranked among the top internationalist business leaders on the basis of his record, to be discussed further in the following chapter.

35

A CLUSTER OF COOPERATING AND COMPETING
INTERESTS

What emerges from the foregoing analysis of major groups and individuals active in private economic diplomacy is a cluster of overlapping interests. The overall interest is to establish an international climate favorable to Japan. This objective is happily vague and can therefore act as a unifying factor that appeals alike to nationalists and internationalists, protectionists and free traders, profit seekers and peace makers. When coming to grips with the question of favorable to whom and for what, one finds underlying interests which are never precisely identical for any two ministries, business associations, or other participant groups. Fortunately for Japan, chaos does not prevail because the Ministry of Foreign Affairs is recognized as the chief coordinator for government, and Keidanren as the chief coordinator for business. Since companies are by definition self-seeking, their interests are played down through the economic/commercial distinction and through emphasis on government and business associations as sponsors and business leaders as participants.

Business leaders have their own separate interests, however, which may be defined as power and prestige resting on a social base, a company base, and an activity base. Private economic deplomacy advances company interests in the long term but we are more interested here in the way it advances individual interests as a component of the business leader's activity base. It provides participants with an opportunity for leadership, higher public visibility, new international contacts, a platform on which to develop and express policy views, the experience and credit of serving in a diplo.:atic capacity, and the opportunity this brings to formulate allies and alliances outside of one's company.

Business leaders vary a great deal in their personal need for, and active participation in, private economic diplomacy. They enhance their careers by it, but are also called upon to participate because they have already reached the top. All we can say to separate the two factors is to suggest a sequence: Achievement within the company comes first, followed by achievement in other fields, building upon one's social, company, and activity bases.

It is important at this point to keep the internationalist business leader in perspective: He represents only a part of the zaikai, the internationalist faction, if you will, which by definition is already a rather small number of men at the top of the business community. He is a very busy man and private economic diplomacy represents only a part of his interests. Finally, the extent of his participation is not necessarily in proportion to his actual influence within the business community or government. His influence can be measured, if at all, only by examining all the remaining components of his activity base together with his social and company bases which are not the concern of this study. It is our concern to abstract from empirical evidence and case studies in the following chapters a clearer idea of how private economic diplomacy serves each of the above interests and how conflicts are resolved. How is it, for example, that Nagano, Iwasa, and Kikawada differ so sharply in personal style and power bases, yet work together in private economic diplomacy, sometimes alternating chairman and vice-chairman roles?* They compete with each other in groups and as individuals for leadership of the business community but they remain close friends.[39] We have borrowed the term cooperative-competition to characterize the set of ground rules by which Japanese resolve various participant interests. We now turn to an examination of four variations of private economic diplomacy.

NOTES

1. Lawrence Olson, Japan in Postwar Asia (New York: Praeger, 1970), p. 71. See also the speech by Ichiro Sato, Director-General, Economic Planning Agency, The Daily Yomiuri, April 29, 1971.
2. Office of the Prime Minister, Bureau of Statistics, Nihon Tokei Nenkan [Japan Statistical Yearbook] (Tokyo: Finance Ministry, 1963), p. 452.
3. Joji Watanuki, Nihon no seiji shakai [Japan's political society] (Tokyo: Tokyo Daigaku Shuppankai, 1967), pp. 105, 111. Watanuki credits Miki Yonosuke, popular economic writer, with coining the term hashutsufu shacho, literally "dispatched housekeeper president," for the bureaucrat turned company president. Watanuki also notes an equally colorful term amakudari shacho ("parachuted president"), and predicts an increase in this type of lateral entry to business, highly desirable as a career pattern.
4. Interviews with Yutaka Kondo and Yasu Murazumi, Economic Affairs Bureau, Ministry of Foreign Affairs, July 1 and August 1, 1968.
5. Interview with Masahisa Segawa, Secretary to the President, The Fuji Bank, Ltd., October 26, 1968. See also Yuichiro Noguchi, "Trends in Thought Among Structural Reformists in Japanese Industry," Journal of Social and Political Ideas in Japan, April 1967, p. 14.

---

*Note particularly the alternating roles of Nagano and Iwasa in the Iwasa mission, Pacific Basin Economic Council, and Private Investment Company for Asia.

6. Japan Times, December 8, 1968, p. 10.

7. For official organization charts of each ministry see White Papers of Japan, 1970-71 (Tokyo: Japan Institute of International Affairs, 1972), pp. 426-49.

8. Interview with Akira Saito, Political Reporter, Mainichi Shimbun, February 24, 1969.

9. Donald C. Hellman, Japanese Domestic Politics and Foreign Policy: The Peace Agreement with the Soviet Union (Berkeley: University of California Press, 1969). Hellman was surprised to find very little cohesive influence by business in his case study.

10. Interview with Setsuo Takashima, Chief, Heavy Industries Bureau, Ministry of International Trade and Industry, September 18, 1968.

11. Interview with Yasu Murazumi, Economic Affairs Bureau, Ministry of Foreign Affairs, August 1, 1968.

12. Interview with Masuo Shibata, International Trade and Planning Section, Ministry of International Trade and Industry, October 18, 1968.

13. Interview with Katsuhiro Fujiwara, United States-Japan Trade Council, January 19, 1973.

14. For a lively account of the new structure policy battles written by a MITI official, see Shigeru Sahashi, Ishoku Kanryo [A unique bureaucracy] (Tokyo: Diamondosha, 1967). See also Noguchi, op. cit., pp. 11-26.

15. Keizai Dantai Rengokai (Japan Federation of Economic Organizations). For background on business associations and their relationship to government, see Chitoshi Yanaga, Big Business in Japanese Politics (Englewood Cliffs, N.J.: Prentice-Hall, 1967), pp. 41-52, passim. Each association also publishes its own history in Japanese, or see Hideo Akimoto, Keidanren (Tokyo: Sekkasha, 1968).

16. Japan Economic Journal, May 25, 1971, p. 20.

17. The Yomiuri, March 25, 1968, p. 5.

18. Interview with Kunio Okabe, Assistant Manager of Foreign Relations, Nippon Steel, March 1, 1969. The man who held this post in 1968 was formerly Consul General in New Orleans.

19. Watanuki, op. cit., p. 104.

20. Japan Times, August 29, 1968, p. 8.

21. Japan Economic Journal, June 15, 1971.

22. See the author's Keizai Doyukai: A Japanese Interest Group, unpublished essay submitted in partial fulfillment of the requirements for the Certificate of the East Asian Institute, Columbia University, 1966.

23. M. Y. Yoshino, Japan's Managerial System (Cambridge, Mass.: M.I.T. Press, 1968), p. 40.

24. See, for example, Research and Policy Committee, East-West Trade: A Common Policy for the West (New York: Committee for Economic Development in association with Keizai Doyukai and CEPES, 1965), and Japan in the Free World Economy (New York: Committee for Economic Development, 1963).

25. Japan Economic Journal, June 1, 1971, p. 20.

26. See Shigeo Nagano's definition in "Zaikaijintte donna hito?" Asahi Shimbun, May 16, 1968. For a more detailed definition see Yukio Suzuki, Gendai Nihon no kenryoku erito [The power elite of contemporary Japan] (Tokyo: Bansho Shobo, 1967), pp. 16ᵣ28.

27. Although differing in substance, the idea for the power base analysis that follows was suggested by the Japanese politician's three "bans" essential to win elections: jiban [an organizational base]; kanban [public image]; kaban [wealth]. See Nobutaka Ike, Japanese Politics (New York: Alfred A. Knopf, 1957), pp. 193, 197, 200.

28. For a description of the extended family clique [keibatsu] and the university clique [gakubatsu] see Yanaga, op. cit., pp. 15-23.

29. Interview with Kiichi Miyazawa, Minister of International Trade and Industry, March 10, 1969. In Miyazawa's opinion, Ataru Kobayashi would have become president of Keidanren in the late 1950s except that he had no legitimate company base, that is, he was not an executive of a company in a basic industry.

30. For a discussion of the internationalist faction and a thorough account of the interplay of business and government political power, see Hideo Akimoto, op. cit., pp. 217, 225. Akimoto describes the postwar shifts in organizational and factional power in the business community with charts and a chronology.

31. Derek Davis, "The Challenge of Japan," Far Eastern Economic Review, January 2, 1971, p. 20.

32. Asahi Evening News, January 17, 1968, and The Yomiuri, March 25, 1968.

33. Japan Economic Journal, January 19, 1971, p. 11.

34. Koji Kanamura in Far Eastern Economic Review, February 20, 1971, p. 37, and April 24, 1971, p. 74.

35. Sangyo Mondai Kenkyukai, abbreviated Sanken. When first organized, Sanken had only nine members and was assumed to be anti-former zaibatsu (Suzuki, op. cit., p. 91.). But gradually it gained a broader identity along with participation by men from the Mitsubishi and Mitsui groups, and heads of all four major business associations. Kikawada is apparently attempting to develop an informal coordinating body of top business leaders which, as such, would compete with Keidanren. For an analysis and brief biographies of Sanken's twenty-four members, see Takeo Kimura, "Sanken," Chuo Koron, July 1971, pp. 166-96.

36. Interview with Kazutaka Kikawada, President, Tokyo Electric Power Company, Inc., March 7, 1969.

37. Yanaga, op. cit., p. 311. The Council is an advisory group under the prime minister's office and consists largely of businessmen. One of its main tasks is to review the national economic plans drafted by the government's Economic Planning Agency.

38. Kobayashi's 1970 income was listed as approximately $548,000, or three to nine times that of Adachi, Nagano, Uemura, Iwasa, and Kikawada. Mainichi Daily News, January 24, 1971.

39. Interview with Yasuo Takeyama, Chief of the Editorial Staff, Nihon Keizai Shimbun, February 18, 1969.

A roving ambassador (ido taishi) may be sent for purposes similar to those of an economic mission, but he differs from such a mission in that he acts as an individual and is appointed by the Foreign Minister. As a general rule he is given a regional assignment and spends relatively little time in any one country. Missions to a region are fairly common, but the roving ambassador was used more expressly as a regional diplomatic instrument. In fact, the main purpose of the roving ambassador approach after its initial use in 1956 was to help implement a new regional emphasis in Japanese diplomacy, an emphasis that included a role for businessmen.* The Foreign Ministry Blue Book of 1958 recognized the new regional concept as official policy.

> In the world economy most recently there are many problems which have common aspects regionally. Consequently, in order to grasp their direction, it is necessary to take an integrated view, not simply of separate countries but from a broader regional viewpoint.[1]

Through the use of businessmen to help implement regional thinking, the Ministry must have hoped to incorporate their suggestions afterward in drafting new economic policies. Each roving ambassadorship was a multipurpose fact-finding mission which required

---

*Senior politicians and scholars have since been sent frequently on roving ambassador assignments by the Prime Minister without appointment by the Foreign Minister (for example, Diet members to the People's Republic of China), but this is another matter not within the scope of the present study.

discussions with many groups within each country. The roving ambassador was expected to meet local government officials and private
citizens, Japanese diplomats, and resident Japanese businessmen as
well.[2]

Once having made its initial contribution to regional thinking
in Japanese diplomacy, the roving ambassador approach was seldom
used and it is not difficult to see why. A single envoy can hardly be
expected to improve the economic climate for Japan in any lasting
way if he must cover seven to thirteen countries in a few weeks. Nor
can he reach as many people at home or abroad as can an economic
mission. The mission undergoes internal consensus-building on policy
matters which it can then present to others as a consensus rather
than the views of a single individual. It is therefore not surprising
that the economic mission for the most part replaced the roving ambassador after 1958. Nevertheless, business leaders as roving ambassadors did have a role to play and we shall briefly sketch the history
of that role, then in one case show how it related to the interests of
the Foreign Ministry and the individual appointee.

Five years after Katsumi Yamagata's precedent-setting tour
to Europe and America in 1951 on behalf of the Yoshida government
and the Japanese shipbuilding industry, Prime Minister Hatoyama
sent Aiichiro Fujiyama to the Philippines to negotiate a reparations
agreement. At the time, Fujiyama was president of Nissho, as well
as chairman of the Japan Commercial Arbitration Association. He
successfully concluded a reparations agreement of $550 million along
with $250 million in commercial loans.[3]

Based on this initial experience in 1956, Fujiyama developed
and applied the roving ambassador concept the following year when
he became foreign minister in the cabinet of Nobusuke Kishi. In the
short space of time from August to September 1957 Fujiyama sent
four prominent businessmen on separate tours as roving ambassadors
(see Table 4).

Of the four roving ambassador appointments in 1957 Ataru
Kobayashi had the special assignment of signing a reparations agreement with Indonesia. Premier Kishi and President Sukarno had agreed
on general terms during brief talks that took place in Djakarta in
November 1957. Kobayashi then initialled the final agreement in
December to be followed by Foreign Minister Fujiyama's signature
the following January.[4] A formal treaty was signed at the same time
under Japan's foreign policy goal of the 1950s to restore normal bilateral relations that had been disrupted by the war, and to conclude
reparations agreements where necessary.

In 1958 Fujiyama sent two more businessmen, and one scholar,
Seiichi Tobata, to South and Southeast Asia, but following Fujiyama's
resignation as foreign minister,[5] a ten-year period elapsed before

TABLE 4

Businessmen as Roving Ambassadors, 1956-68

Date	Name and Position	Place	Remarks
4/17/56	Fujiyama, Aiichiro Pres., Nissho	Philippines	Negotiated reparations
8/10/57- 10/12/57	Shibusawa, Keizo Ch., Kokusai Denshin Denwa (communications)	South America	Mexico, Uruguay, Argentina, Paraguay, Chile, Bolivia, Panama, Colombia, Venezuela, Dominican Republic, Cuba
8/21/57- 10/11/57	Kobayashi, Ataru Pres., Japan Development Bank	South Asia	Thailand, Burma, Pakistan, India, Ceylon, Singapore, Indonesia, Vietnam, Cambodia, Philippines, Hong Kong; Initialed Indonesian reparations agreement
9/10/57- 10/26/57	Ito, Takeo Pres., OSK Line	Near & Middle East	Egypt, Syria, Iraq, Ethiopia, Sudan, Saudi Arabia, Lebanon, Jordan, Turkey, Iran
9/20/57- 11/16/57	Hotta, Shozo Pres., Sumitomo Bank	Western Europe	Denmark, Sweden, Germany, Switzerland, Austria, England, Belgium, France, Spain, Italy, Greece, Yugoslavia, Israel
1/1/58	Uemura, Kogoro V. Pres., Keidanren	South Vietnam	Unsuccessful in reparations talks
9/5/58	Nagano, Shigeo Pres., Fuji Iron & Steel	Northern & Eastern Europe	USSR, Poland, Czechoslavakia, Denmark, Finland, Norway, Sweden
10/12/67- 11/5/67	Kobayashi, Ataru Pres., Arabian Oil	Central & South America	Mexico, Venezuela, Peru, Argentina, Paraguay, Brazil, United States.

Source: Ministry of Foreign Affairs, Waga gaiko no kinkyo [Present state of our foreign relations] (Tokyo: Ministry of Finance, August 13, 1958), p. 152; Japan Times, August 13, 1958; "Kobayashi Ataru Taishi ikko no Chunam Bei rokkakoku shuccho hokoku" [Report of Ambassador Ataru Kobayashi and his delegation to six countries of Central and South America] (Tokyo: Central and South America Emigration Bureau, Ministry of Foreign Affairs, December 1967).

another businessman was appointed as roving ambassador. This revival occurred in 1967 when Ataru Kobayashi, who had been sent to South Asia in 1957, was appointed to reassess Japan's economic relations with Latin America. Kobayashi's two assignments allow us to focus on him as a case study to illustrate the role and limitations of this form of private economic diplomacy and to probe the group and individual interests which underlie it.

ATARU KOBAYASHI AS ROVING AMBASSADOR AND BUSINESS LEADER

Building on the character sketch of Kobayashi in the previous chapter, we will divide his postwar career into three periods, using the status of his company base as a criterion.

Kobayashi served as president of the Japan Development Bank from 1951 to 1957. It was Premier Shigeru Yoshida who nominated him to head this government chartered bank that makes loans to private industry, a legitimate company base with international scope. During this period Kobayashi established himself among business and political circles as an independent but influential thinker.[6] Part of the independence may have been involuntary since Kobayashi was never fully accepted by former zaibatsu circles because of his relatively weak company and social bases in the prewar period. But politicians do not require pedigrees and within the 1951-57 period Kobayashi became important enough politically to lead at least part of the business community in demanding the immediate resignation of Prime Minister Ichiro Hatoyama in 1956.[7] Hatoyama did resign but not until December 23, after he had normalized relations with the Soviet Union. If neither Kobayashi nor any other business leader was all powerful during 1951-57, at least he was able to place his name at the forefront of business opposition to Hatoyama, to build on his company base, and to gain recognition as a mediator between political and business circles. His appointment as roving ambassador came at the end of this period of establishing his position. Coming as it did under Premier Kishi through Foreign Minister Fujiyama, a businessman, it represented a recognition of Kobayashi's status, both as a political-business go-between and, as president of the Japan Development Bank, a person knowledgeable on international development. Along the way, Kobayashi had been appointed Chairman of the Economic Cooperation Council in 1953 and Counsellor to MITI in 1954. The 1957 roving ambassadorship ended the company base period and began a new period, even more busy politically than 1951-57.

In 1958-67 Kobayashi concentrated on political activities in conjunction with his postwar business comrades-in-arms, the Kobayashi

44

group.[8] His group and individual fortunes rose and fell accordingly. The Kobayashi group, shortened to Kobachu by an intentional misreading of the Chinese character for Ataru, was also called at various times the powerful business faction (jitsuryokuha).[9] It consisted of close friends, including Takeshi Sakurada (Chairman Nisshin Spinning); Shigeo Mizuno (President, Sankei Newspaper); Hiroyuki Imazato (President, Nippon Seiko); Nobutaka Shikanai (President, Fuji Television); and Shigeo Nagano (President, Fuji Iron and Steel). In view of the newness of these leaders relative to prewar zaibatsu firms, coupled with the low prestige of the mass media backgrounds of Mizuno and Shikanai (on the opposite end of the scale from heavy industry), it is not unnatural for this group to be considered antimainstream within the business community, even though its members held leadership positions at Nikkeiren.

Despite divisions within the business community, the Kobayashi group remained influential during the Kishi administration and reached its peak in the administration of Premier Hayato Ikeda, 1960-64.[10] As political advisers and fund raisers to Ikeda, the popular label of "four emperors" for the business leaders above was perhaps appropriate. They were key members in one of Ikeda's informal support groups, the Tuesday Society (Kayokai), which also included Reinosuke Kan and Kazutaka Kikawada from Tokyo Electric Power.[11] During this period Kobayashi maintained his activity base as permanent director of Nikkeiren, chairman of the Overseas Technical Cooperation Agency, and chairman of the Asian Economic Research Institute, an organization sponsored by the business community. Finally, in 1964 the influence of the Kobayashi group declined when Premier Ikeda was succeeded by Eisaku Sato who had his own business support organizations and individual favorities.[12] It became time for Kobayashi to reestablish a company base and begin a new period in his career. Once again the two periods were interspersed with a roving ambassador assignment, this time to six countries in Central and South America in 1967.

From 1968 on, Kobayashi continued his international development interests from a new company base as president of Arabian Oil Company. He had been a director and was asked by Taizo Ishizaka to take over the presidency after Ishizaka had held it briefly in 1967 before becoming chairman of the board. He also maintained his activity base through chairing two important Finance Ministry deliberation councils, Foreign Investment and Finance, although he was never to regain the prominence in political circles that he enjoyed under Premier Ikeda.

The 1967 roving ambassador assignment again symbolized recognition on the government's part of Kobayashi's status as fund raiser and mediator for political circles, on the one hand, and adviser-backer of international development for the Foreign Ministry, on the other. This example places the significance of the roving ambassador at more than a sinecure or figurehead but less than a means to higher status in business circles. It proved more useful to the individual who decided to move horizontally from business to political circles which Kobayashi, and even more so Fujiyama, proceeded to do. Otherwise it was a sign of recognition of one's existing prestige within the business community, hence of one's potential personal utility as an ally of the Foreign Ministry.

Kobayashi's usefulness to the Foreign Ministry in the 1967 appointment lay less with his relationship to the Sato administration than his lengthy experience with developing countries coupled with his standing as a business leader. The group interests surrounding Kobayashi's appointment can be seen from the list of agencies represented on the trip: the Foreign Ministry (Economic Affairs Bureau, Latin American Division); the Export-Import Bank; Institute of Developing Economies (Ajia Keizai Kenkyujo); and the Overseas Technical Cooperation Agency. The Foreign Ministry, with the support of the other agencies represented, stood to gain from (1) whatever favorable climate Kobayashi was able to generate in the countries visited; (2) information gathered on the region as a whole as recorded in the Kobayashi Report; [13] (3) policy development and support vis-a-vis other ministries and political and business circles on the question of Latin America as a market for Japanese assistance, investments, and exports.

The Kobayashi Report was in fact a plea for more Japanese investment in Latin America. It warned that Japan was falling behind the United States and Western Europe in Capital investment [14] and omitted the standard caveats on lack of social infrastructure and managerial development. Kobayashi argued strongly that in Latin America aid and investment by private enterprise rather than the Japanese government should be sufficient because the commcerial base and standard of living were higher than in most other developing regions. He was somewhat reserved concerning the dangers of inflation and political instability but he remained bullish, documenting improvements in these areas too for 1963-67. He noted that as of 1967 Latin America was the leading region for Japanese overseas investment (29 percent compared to 25 percent for second place North America), and concluded that further investment was highly desirable. He recommended an expansion of economic research, technological assistance, natural resources surveys, capital investment, and cooperation with international agencies, arguing that returns would be realized not only in investment profits, but also in expanded sources of raw materials and enlarged export markets. [15]

On reading the Kobayashi Report one is struck by the intensity with which he is communicating a policy position to Japanese readers, quite unlike random information-gathering, public relations, or other diplomatic objectives. The domestic dialogue over economic policy stands at least as important as impacts toward a favorable climate in the host countries. This is borne out by Kobayashi's itinerary which, in keeping with a roving ambassador's responsibilities, frequently included visits with Japanese residents abroad.[16] And if Kobayashi is considered here in his earlier political role as a government-business mediator, then it becomes a case of the Foreign Ministry telling the business community (through Kobayashi) that it should greatly increase its investment in Latin America, but that the burden of accompanying aid programs should be borne by the private sector more than government, that is, the Foreign Ministry.

Thus in assessing each type of private economic diplomacy one should not overlook the internal or domestic dimension which proceeds during and after the event. The term "diplomacy" fails to connote that what takes place abroad becomes supporting evidence for contending economic policies and groups at home. Kobayashi's tour on the level of domestic politics can be viewed as an instrument for rallying support—at home and abroad—for a particular policy toward investment in America from the point of view of an internationalist business leader.*

SIGNIFICANCE OF ROVING AMBASSADORS

As a developmental step in Japanese diplomacy and in an individual's career, the roving ambassador device proved useful; as a diplomatic instrument it had limited use and impact. The effective roving ambassador can gain a sense of the problems common to a region and can demonstrate a positive attitude toward their solution, both during his tour and upon his return, but any lasting impact would require both the use of other forms of diplomacy and a business leader with considerable domestic influence. Shigeo Nagano's early assignment to the Soviet Union as a roving ambassador became one of a long series of steps leading to the Japan-Soviet Joint Business Cooperation Committee in which Nagano remained quite active.[17] When so viewed as one of a series of diplomatic initiatives, the roving ambassador device served its modest purpose as a regional supplement to

----

*Kobayashi has been a consistent proponent of trade and capital liberalization through his chairmanship of the Foreign Investment Council. His background also speaks for his international perspective: presidencies of Overseas Technical Cooperation Agency, Japan Development Bank, and the Arabian Oil Company.

professional diplomacy but its future use will depend on the type of diplomatic problem and personalities available.

From the individual's point of view an appointment as roving ambassador will certainly strengthen his activity base, but economic missions can do the same thing for more businessmen with more impact.

NOTES

1. Ministry of Foreign Affairs, ed., Waga gaiko no kinkyo [Present state of our foreign relations] (Tokyo: Ministry of Finance, 1958), p. 152.

2. Ibid.

3. Japan Quarterly, Vol. 3 (1956), p. 393.

4. Japan Quarterly, Vol. 5 (1958), pp. 130, 264.

5. Our data show three instances of Fujiyama's leadership in private economic diplomacy (Appendix A) but all occurred early in the 1956-68 period. In terms of our three bases of power, since serving as foreign minister, Fujiyama gave up his company base, and his activity base became wholly political. As a member of the Diet, Fujiyama has been a contender for the presidency of the Liberal-Democratic Party and an outspoken leader in the movement for rapprochement with the People's Republic of China, but he does not have solid support from the business community he left. Chitoshi Yanaga, Big Business in Japanese Politics (New Haven, Conn.: Yale University Press, 1968), pp. 148-51.

6. Hideo Akimoto, Keidanren [Federation of Economic Organizations] (Tokyo: Sekkasha, 1968), pp. 163, 183, especially pp. 180-83, or Yoshinori Kato, Zaikai [Big business circles] (Tokyo: Kawada Shobo Shinsha, 1966), pp. 109-11, 154-61.

7. Akira Sakaguchi, "The Power of the Financial World in Politics," Journal of Social and Political Ideas in Japan, December 1964, pp. 115-19.

8. Akimoto, op. cit., p. 183, and The Yomiuri, February 8, 1968.

9. Yuichiro Noguchi, "Trends in Thought Among Structural Reformists in Japanese Industry," Journal of Social and Political Ideas in Japan, December 1964, p. 25, and Yukio Suzuki, Gendai Nihonno Kenryoku erito [The power elite of contemporary Japan] (Tokyo: Bansho Shobo, 1967), p. 91.

10. "Zaikai no Ikeda sanmyaku" [The Ikeda groups in big business], Shukan Asahi, October 30, 1960, pp. 5-13.

11. Joji Watanuki, Nihon no seiji shakai [Japan's Political Society] (Tokyo: Tokyo Daigaku Shuppankai, 1967), p. 106.

12. Nagano and Kikawada managed to retain their positions politically close to the new premier, Eisaku Sato, who favored a large number of support organizations with which he met often but not with quite the intimacy that Premier Ikeda maintained with business leaders. Interview with Koji Hiroshima, Assistant to the President, Marubeni-Iida Company, Ltd., March 6, 1969. See also Joji Watanuki, ibid., p. 104.

13. "Kobayashi Ataru Taishi ikko no Chunam Bei rokkakoku shuccho hokoku" [Report of Ambassador Ataru Kobayashi and his delegation to six countries of Central and South America] (Tokyo: Gaimusho Chunam Bei Iminkyoku, December 1967).

14. Ibid., p. 39.

15. Ibid., pp. 2-10.

16. During his two days in Mexico, for example, Kobayashi visited Matsushita Electric, Toshiba and Nissan Automobile plants; dined with representatives of Mitsui, Mitsubishi, C. Itoh and Marubeni Iida trading companies, and the Bank of Tokyo. In Argentina he visited a Japanese emigrant settlement and the Japan Woolen Goods Company, attended a Japan-Argentina Joint Economic Committee meeting, dined with the Japanese Ambassador, and talked with the Argentine Economic and Foreign Ministers. Ibid., pp. 43, 45.

17. Shigeo Nagano, "Russo-Japanese Trade," Japan Quarterly 14 (October-December 1967), pp. 422-28. Nagano led a steel industry mission to the Soviet Union in June 1965 and at the request of Ishizaka and Adachi, took the opportunity to respond to an earlier Soviet initiative by proposing the joint economic committee form to further Japan-Soviet economic cooperation. Economic missions to the Soviet Union also contributed to the formulation of the joint committee (Chapter 5), all indicative of how different forms of private economic diplomacy combine over time to supplement professional diplomacy.

CHAPTER
4
ECONOMIC MISSIONS

The most commonly used agency through which private economic diplomacy is conducted is the economic mission (keizai shisetsudan). It may be sponsored by government or business but it is defined by its objective, which is to establish or maintain a favorable climate for the expansion of Japanese trade, aid, or investment. It is characterized by a careful selection process, policy discussions with top officials and businessmen of the host country, and a report which reflects a consensus of mission members on policy recommendations. A commercial mission may precede, but ideally follows, the economic mission and may conclude specific trade arrangements. The Japanese attempt to separate the two functions on the ground that if the economic/commercial distinction were not maintained, the commercial mission's focus on sales would become an obstacle in achieving the economic mission's diplomatic objectives.[1]

The purpose of this chapter is to show how an economic mission goes about achieving its objectives—through selection, coordination, and follow-up phases—and how this relates to the satisfaction of group and individual interests which are represented on the mission.

Within the overall objective of a favorable economic climate, the economic mission may also attempt to: (1) improve Japan's image abroad; (2) give special attention to selected countries and regions; (3) remove obstacles to trade and investment; (4) negotiate agreements; and (5) gather information and formulate policy recommendations.

The mix of these objectives varies widely. A government-sponsored mission to Central America removed the obstacle of Guatemala's discriminatory treatment of imports from Japan and it concluded commercial agreements with El Salvador and Mexico.[2] A mission to Burma in 1960 negotiated Japanese rice imports under a rapidly deteriorating local situation.[3] In Malaysia a mission served

50

the information-gathering function by confirming the stability of the new government in 1962.[4] For an example of the overall objective of a favorable climate, we shall focus on a single economic mission, the Takasugi mission to Indonesia in 1968.[5]

The return of Japanese investment to Indonesia after economic relations had virtually ceased under the Sukarno regime began in 1967 when the Suharto government announced a new policy to welcome foreign capital. In that year Nagano, Iwasa, and Masao Anzai, among others, attended a conference at Djakarta of business executives from fourteen nations.[6] They reported to Keidanren's Standing Committee on Economic Cooperation in no uncertain terms: Japan should invest in Indonesia in a coordinated manner but swiftly and heavily, with joint ventures, technical assistance, and loans.

The reasons for their sense of urgency are partially discernible in the scale of foreign investment in Indonesia in 1967-68. By country, the United States had nineteen projects, the Netherlands fourteen, Hong Kong thirteen, Japan twelve, and others had three to five projects. But more important is the comparison of total intended capital investment. Here the United States led with approximately $120 million followed by Canada, Korea, the Netherlands, and Japan,[7] despite the fact that Japan ranked second on this list in gross national product.

The first remedial step taken by business circles was to establish a new Keidanren standing committee on Indonesia for the purpose of coordinating Japan's private business projects there. Shinichi Takasugi, advisor and former chairman of Mitsubishi Electric, was appointed to head the new committee.[8]

The first government step, in cooperation with Keidanren, was to sponsor an economic mission. Upon announcement of the mission, the Asahi Shimbun observed, "Recently in Indonesia, one can say there has been a rush of economic missions from every country."[9] The Takasugi Mission, then, was conceived in an atmosphere of urgency in which a strong effort would be needed for Japan to catch up in investment, aid, and trade.

The climate problem in Indonesia was to reestablish an atmosphere of mutual trust, to convince the Indonesians of Japan's sincere interest in cooperating with the new Suharto government on development projects which would benefit both Indonesia and Japan. A secondary objective of the mission was to awaken Japan domestically to the importance of Indonesia and to its readiness to fruitfully take on Japanese trade, aid, and development projects.[10]

Within the framework of establishing a better investment atmosphere, the mission attempted to deal with specific obstacles to trade and investment: an inadequate foreign assistance program to Indonesia; lack of an investment guarantee arrangement; sluggish approval procedures on both sides; heavy taxation of joint ventures; and lack of a middle management class in Indonesia to carry out planning and projects after major policy decisions have been made at the top.

SELECTION OF PERSONNEL

The primary method of achieving the mission's objectives is in selecting men appropriate to each mission. Ideally this means sending business leaders appropriate to the host country and at the same time capable of representing the interests of Japan rather than their companies alone. First, the chairman of a mission is appointed by the Foreign Ministry or sponsoring business association, depending on whether the mission is sponsored by government or business. Next, the mission chairman normally selects the members through consultation with his colleagues, with the appropriate business association committee, and with the Vice-Minister of Foreign Affairs. The criteria include: (1) major industrial groups should be represented; (2) no single industrial group should dominate;[11] (3) industries with interests in the host country, but not necessarily companies, should be represented; and (4) the ability and prestige of each member should be sufficiently high to represent Japan in the host country.

As chairman of Keidanren's Committee on Indonesia, Takasugi was appointed by the Foreign Ministry to head the mission.* He and his committee were then responsible for selecting members of the mission, a task which proved rather difficult.[12] Since one of the mission's objectives was to educate Japanese leaders and the public about the new situation in Indonesia, membership should have included men with strong domestic influence in Japan, as opposed to selection only for effectiveness within the target country. Moreoever, many companies wanted to be represented in the new approach to Indonesia. Takasugi's response to these pressures was to propose sending a mission of one hundred members based on nominations from seven industry subcommittees of the Committee on Indonesia. Iwasa was opposed, arguing that fifteen carefully selected men could better solve the problem. Iwasa further believed that economic mission members should not have special interests in Indonesia. The Economic Affairs Bureau of the Foreign Ministry also favored a small mission without special interests, since the Indonesian government had requested economic negotiations and development advice in general, not discussions of

---

*As former chairman and president of Mitsubishi Electric, Takasugi had the necessary company base, and as chairman of the Committee on Indonesia he had a favorable activity base to head the mission. He had also led earlier missions to Malaysia and Korea.

specific projects by those who might actually set up, for example, fertilizer or power plants. These should be promoted on separate commercial missions. Both Indonesian and Japanese authorities being in agreement on this point, the first list of mission members was thrown out. The final list consisted of fourteen top executives including Iwasa as vice-chairman, and, among others, Shigeo Nagano, Toshio Doko, and Masao Anzai (presidents of Fuji Iron and Steel, Toshiba, and Showa Denko, respectively, all regularly active in private economic diplomacy). Thus the mission more than merits the label of major (ogata) which refers not to size but to caliber of members—all business leaders.[13]

After the chairman and members of a mission are chosen, appropriate ministries are invited to send official advisers on the mission. There are several reasons for this: (1) advisers can provide official information in their area of expertise for the benefit of the diplomatic laymen members; (2) the mission's policy statements can be kept closer to a line felt desirable by the participating ministry; and (3) both business members and government advisers can perform a watchdog function by observing diplomatic posts abroad and by reporting on their effectiveness to the Foreign Ministry. In at least one case a consul-general was transferred upon recommendation of mission members.[14]

Candidates for advisers were also in abundance. The Foreign Ministry originally invited MITI, the Economic Planning Agency, the Agriculture and Forestry Ministry, and the Finance Ministry, as well as the Japan Export-Import Bank and the Overseas Economic Cooperation Agency. The latter two declined, perhaps because each government agency must fund its own representative. The other five agencies sent advisers as follows: Counsellor, Minister's Secretariat, Ministry of Finance; Chief, Asia Division, Economic Affairs Bureau, Ministry of Foreign Affairs; Chief, Economic Cooperation Policy Section, Economic Cooperation Division, Trade & Development Bureau, MITI; Chief, Economic Cooperation Section, Coordination Bureau, Economic Planning Agency; Acting Chief, International Cooperation Branch, International Division, Agriculture & Forestry Economic Bureau, Ministry of Agriculture & Forestry; Secretary, Planning Division, Economic Cooperation Bureau, Ministry of Foreign Affairs.[15]

COORDINATION

Another method of achieving the mission's objectives is coordination—the task of the sponsor or chief sponsor—between the business associations and the Foreign Ministry for the government. Coordination, before and after a mission, is carried on by telephone, meetings, or memoranda among all the interested parties, most frequently at the division chief level. The division chief, often accompanied by his assistant, may visit the office of a mission member to gain his advice and/or approval on a particular policy position. If the member is quite senior or otherwise unavailable, the system works just as well by utilizing the member's assistant who then explains the position to the member. The member may then call the chairman of the mission, business association colleagues, his trade federation, or any number of interested parties, but often the assistant's arguments can be decisive since it is his job to be up to date on where other parties stand on an issue, and why. If no agreement is reached on what position the mission should take on a particular issue, the dialogue is advanced to the next level. This process on rare occasions reaches as far as the vice-minister or minister level. The relative strength of each party is not fixed, but depends on the extent of each party's interest in the issue at hand.

One of the Takasugi mission issues was the Indonesian demand that all foreign companies should pay a fee for the privilege of undertaking each development project. Japanese companies and MITI had a strong interest in this while the Foreign Ministry had a lesser interest and would act as an arbitrator as well. The mission argued successfully against payment of any fee by individual companies on a project basis.

The coordination for such policies in this case was the collective responsibility of the advisers appointed to the mission by four ministries and the Economic Planning Agency, with the two Foreign Ministry advisers having overall responsibility.

The coordination of the itinerary was also the job of the staff of the sponsoring agency, the Foreign Ministry in the case of the Takasugi mission. Reservations and appointments are all made in advance through the local embassy or consulate. An economic mission aims at the highest possible level of government and business in the host country. This focus on elites has the dual advantage of reaching those individuals responsible for policy and decision-making, and facilitating the recruitment of the best Japanese business leaders. This is the reason that a mission to the United States, for example, will invariably include Washington, D.C., in the itinerary, and if possible, talks with cabinet level officials and members of Congress.

The Takasugi mission's itinerary aimed at high level discussions with Indonesian leaders and planners, including an hour and a half in two discussions with President Suharto. The level had to be high, for the Indonesians were prepared to outline in detail their future economic program for both government and private industry. The Japanese for their part had to ask the right questions of the right people to determine if the climate and conditions were indeed right

for a major Japanese investment in Indonesia. A key man in these
talks was Hamengku Buwono, State Minister of Economy, Finance,
and Industry. Visits with Buwono were scheduled on at least three
different days in one form or another.

Behind the discussions, receptions, visits to dams, and so forth,
the staff assistants for each mission member also played a role. In
addition to drafting speeches and interpreting for members whose
English is inadequate, these assistants are kept busy with the inevit-
able problems of luggage, transportation, gifts, and other errands.
Their presence on the mission is perhaps another distinguishing feature of Japanese private economic diplomacy and it causes problems
by nearly doubling the size of the mission. Eleven of fourteen business members of the Takasugi mission brought personal assistants,
and the Keidanren mission member brought two research assistants
for a total of thirteen. This slows processing of luggage, transportation, and customs inspection considerably, since only the mission
chairman, vice-chairman, and government advisers on a government
sponsored mission have diplomatic passports. In addition, the members' assistants must handle such items as the seventy-five gift foun-
tain pens, not to mention the 900 bottles of mineral water that were
brought along on the Takasugi mission to ensure the health of the
more elderly members. The appearance of all that manpower, luggage, and cartons of mineral water descending upon Djakarta can
hardly have contributed to the objective of a favorable climate, so
important to this particular mission.

In the coordination of funding a government sponsored mission,
the Foreign Ministry again has ultimate responsibility, although a
sponsoring business association may collect and disperse funds for
participating companies. The Foreign Ministry pays the personal
expenses of the mission leader as well as his obligatory social expenses, that is, a reception and dinner given by the mission for the
host country. On the Takasugi mission, the Foreign Ministry put up
approximately $3,000. This covered all of Chairman Takasugi's ex-
penses including local transportation for the mission consisting of
ten rental cars for the entire group of thirty-six.

The Ministry may also pay for publication of the mission report.
Expenses of the individual members—transportation, lodging, meals—
must be paid by them, that is, by their companies. A mission fund
of $6,580, collected from the Takasugi members' companies by
Keidanren, was budgeted to include expenses of the nongovernmental
advisers, in this case a Keidanren adviser and a Tokyo University
professor. The expenses of the three secretarial staff men were
paid directly by Keidanren. Each company's share came to just under
$440 plus the individual member's expenses, a total cost which is
more than justified by the benefit to the company in public relations,

not to mention later business based on the personal relationships established through the mission.

The companies must also absorb the costs of members' assistants who accompany the mission, and any special advisers (scholars, labor leaders, journalists) who are not covered by government funds. Coordination of the mission's composition, and policy positions funds, among interested parties places a premium on cooperation between business and government groups and on their ability to reach a consensus and abide by it.

FOLLOW-UP

Follow-up is the final method of achieving the mission's objectives. The written report provides the most visible form of follow-up—it may be elaborately published with lengthy data as part of the mission's information-gathering function—and specific recommendations to government and business.* Of course what a report recommends and what is actually done are not necessarily identical or even closely similar. One observer at least, was doubtful whether any mission recommendations are incorporated into government policy in a direct cause and effect manner.[16] Rather, mission reports tend to reflect views held by business leaders after liaison with the appropriate ministries and political circles.

Nonwritten follow-up consists in consensus-building discussions toward drafting the written report and actions taken by mission participants individually or by sponsoring groups. Frequently follow-up takes the form of establishing a liaison channel—a joint committee or conference—to continue the dialogue begun by the mission, to coordinate the ventures of Japanese companies, or to apply pressure toward removing particular obstacles to trade and investment. The thrust of such follow-up is to move from the general tone of the economic mission to specific measures, from mutual trust to joint ventures and the like.

The Takasugi Report's policy recommendations aimed first at the Japanese government and second at the Japanese business community†. The report's significance is suggested by the extra time

---

*The Takasugi report contained considerable factual data on Indonesian industry and governmental structure including eleven elaborate fold out charts. Most mission reports provide this type of information.

†The report contains a preface by Takasugi, the itinerary and list of members, and a text in three sections: general remarks and

and care devoted to its publication on May 25, 1969, almost eight months after the mission. Most of this time was spent on cross-checking the draft between Keidanren and the Foreign Ministry at the division chief level.

The Fuji Bank should also be mentioned as a third party because of the responsibility carried by Iwasa as vice-chairman of the mission and his assistant, Masahisa Segawa. Other individuals who worked together in drafting the report were the Senior Managing Director of Keidanren, the Assistant Chief Foreign Manager of Fuji Bank, and the Chief of the Asia Division, Economic Affairs Bureau, Ministry of Foreign Affairs. They had the unenviable task of drafting, hand carrying to each office, discussing with each participant, and redrafting until a consensus was reached. Eight members added separate statements of their own to the report. Thus their problem was to build as broad a consensus as possible from three sets of opinion: the official position of Japan and Indonesia (paramount in the report), an unofficial consensus, and individual impressions.

The recommendations section presented a general statement of what official policy should be, followed by specific recommendations to implement policy.[17] It began by recognizing the unpleasant fact that Indonesia will require large amounts of assistance for several years. Then it reported favorably on Indonesia's five-year plan which assigns top priority to agriculture and the control of inflation. It pronounced the plan feasible in terms of target figures and observed that a major portion of the planned capital investment must come from foreign sources. The recommendation concluded that Japan should cooperate in the realization of the five-year plan, and the justification given for the cooperation was rather interesting: "If we hold back on capital and economic assistance to Indonesia, Japan is in danger of losing the opportunity to invest in Indonesia. If you think how very close Japan is to the resources of Indonesia we must take on investment and economic assistance to Indonesia with a forward-looking attitude."[18] There was no attempt to present altruistic or moral reasons for helping Indonesia. Although the language of the report was quite tactful (for example, "advise" and "cooperate with" are used in preference to "teach"), its message was urgent: Unless immediate cooperative steps are taken, Japan will "lose out" in Indonesia, lose a close source of raw materials and a market for Japanese exports.

---

recommendations, details, and a supplement which contains one report to Foreign Minister Takeo Miki, another for Keidanren, press conference, and individual statements.

Was the Takasugi mission successful in establishing a climate of mutual trust? The majority view of Takasugi mission members at the time was that it was a qualified success. It "opened the gates" for increased economic activity between the two countries;[19] it established the necessary personal relationships and follow-up committees; the Japanese reassured themselves of Indonesian stability; the Indonesians learned that prior slowness on the part of the Japanese was not due to lack of interest. Further, it resulted in increased aid to Indonesia and a flurry of joint venture and investment activity by Japan, with efforts to cut down approval time. We shall take a closer look at these results in terms of the interests of the mission's sponsors and participants.

UNDERLYING INTERESTS

The Foreign Ministry was the first to benefit from the mission, for the government faced an immediate policy decision on aid to Indonesia. Views and information gathered by the Takasugi mission were put to use with uncommon speed (apart from the report itself), when the Intergovernmental Group on Indonesia (IGGI), which consists of donor nations as members, held one of its periodic meetings in the Netherlands on October 21-23, 1968, less than two weeks after the Takasugi mission returned home. The mission's support was needed because, after requests of $200 million in 1967, and over $300 million in 1968, Indonesia was asking for $500 million in 1969. An advance press commentary said, "Indonesia faces a tough fight to obtain the money it needs, since some nations, particularly Japan, have found it difficult to justify giving the aid requested from them in the past."[20]

This time there was sufficient support to more than justify Japanese aid. Takasugi had reported in detail to the Foreign Ministry on such matters as priority industries, including bicycles and truck assembly. Economist Saburo Okita had also reported to the Ministry at the same time, but in a separate capacity. He predicted that Indonesia will need economic aid for the next fifteen years and that the amounts will continue to increase at least during the next five years.[21] By combining the details of the Takasugi and Okita up-to-the-minute reports with its own diplomatic dispatches, the Foreign Ministry was well prepared for the IGGI conference and bilateral negotiations which continued after 1968. Furthermore, the Ministry had been careful to include a Finance Ministry representative as an advisor to the mission, a Counsellor from the Finance Ministry Secretariat. This meant that a policy consensus of the mission would be supported by Finance since, by preconsultation, Finance became a part of the consensus. Soon after the IGGI conference Japan signed a loan to Indonesia for $110 million.[22]

In the private sector the Takasugi mission established a permanent channel for liaison on joint problems of Indonesian and Japanese private enterprise. The Indonesians agreed to set up a liaison mission in Djakarta to coordinate Japanese investment moves from Tokyo and to concentrate on labor and productivity weaknesses. The Japanese already had their own business liaison organ in the Keidanren Committee on Indonesia. They also explained plans to set up a Private Investment Company for Asia which could become a major source of foreign investment for Indonesians. Once the necessary organs for liaison were agreed upon, talks then took the direction of case by case discussion of industrial sectors.

In the forest products industry, the mission obtained agreement in principle from the Indonesian government for a joint Japanese-Indonesian consultation committee in charge of general development of Indonesia's forestry resources.[23] This is a manifestation of Japan's urge to coordinate its own efforts to avoid excessive competition and to organize against losing out to foreign companies, or at least to "solve possible conflicts of interest with similar attempts in Indonesia by other nations."[24] The committee functions on the Japanese side as a unit of Keidanren; it was expected to become a regular consultation organ between government and industrial representatives of both countries. It supervises timber ventures by various companies, keeps records for general information, and makes recommendations to solve various joint venture problems.

Company interests were well served by the Takasugi Mission, as might be expected, with two qualifying features. First, since it was an economic mission no contracts could be signed on the mission. Second, by mutual agreement, projects were discussed on the basis of a consortium of Japanese companies. This was to avoid the chance for a single company represented on the mission to gain exclusive advantage in Indonesia, a condition which had prevailed in the days of the Sukarno administration.

On these terms, immediately after the Takasugi mission, Japan concluded the biggest forestry agreement Indonesia had ever signed with a foreign investor. Japan's Forestry Development Company, a consortium of companies from Mitsui, Mitsubishi, and Sumitomo groups plus thirty-one other companies, signed a twenty-year contract with Indonesia's state-owned timber company, P. N. Perhutani, to cut logs in eastern Borneo.[25]

In the textile industry, one of the priority industries for which Indonesia welcomed foreign investment, four point ventures eventually grew out of discussions initiated on the Takasugi mission. These were divided by product specialty: polyester rayon, C. Itoh and Mitsui; polyester cotton, Kanematsu; knitting, Mitsui group; weaving, Marubeni-Iida trading. All four joint ventures were to be coordinated by the Keidanren Committee on Indonesia.

In the fertilizer industry the mission also prepared the way for commercial agreements. Masao Anzai, president of Showa Denko and a member of the mission, announced soon after the mission that an agreement had been negotiated between the Japan Ammonium Sulphate Industry Association and the Indonesian government.[26] He also said that Japanese fertilizer makers would strongly press the Foreign Ministry to consider the extension of aid to Indonesia in the form of fertilizers. Here we have a case of common interests of mission members and the host country by which they can combine to put pressure on skeptics within the Japanese government. In this sense it would be incorrect to say that a government sponsored economic mission always represents official government policy, nor is the mission necessarily a protagonist of the host government. Sometimes the mission's role is to muster support to encourage either or both governments to move closer together more quickly, or toward policy directions which for one reason or another they have been slow in assuming.

Individual interests were served on the Takasugi Mission by the personal relationships it helped to establish. This is one of the most important functions of private economic diplomacy, and especially so in Indonesia. To deal with business or government in Indonesia it was considered essential to know top officials because of the lack of a middle management class and the presence of a system which discourages both communication across departmental lines and delegation of responsibility downward. Decisions were made at the top on the basis of personal judgment more than on staff analysis.[27]

The Takasugi Mission provided an opportunity to establish a working relationship with key men in the Suharto administration. It is instructive then, to view the economic mission as a major link in a chain of personal relationships that can be most useful upon reaching such positions of influence as Anzai, Iwasa, Nagano, and others have reached. Let us see how such a chain worked for one of the mission members.

Masao Anzai offers a classic case of strength in all three career bases we discussed in Chapter 2. His social base included a business leader brother, Hiroshi Anzai of Tokyo Gas; a sister married to premier aspirant Takeo Miki; a son who married the sister of Crown Princess Michiko; and other blood relations to the Sumitomo industrial group, Iwasa, and to former Premier Sato. He was also a member of Choeikai, Premier Sato's support group of business leaders.[28]

Anzai's company base was as president of Showa Denko, a large chemical company and a perfect example of a prestigious heavy industry. In 1971 Anzai moved to the chairman post where he remained active in company and non-company affairs.

Keidanren served as Anzai's major activity base where he held key committee chairmanships, including the Economic Cooperation Committee and the Japan-East Germany Economic Committee. Although starting a bit later in private economic diplomacy than some of his colleagues listed in Table 1, Anzai accelerated this component of his activity base. He attended the 1967 Djakarta Conference along with Iwasa and Nagano. He then reappeared as an important member of the Takasugi mission and immediately afterward announced a major joint venture for a consortium of Japanese fertilizer manufacturers. Finally, when Takasugi was appointed by Premier Sato to head the Overseas Economic Cooperation Agency, Anzai replaced him as chairman of the Indonesia Committee of Keidanren.[29]

An economic mission, therefore, must be considered at the domestic level as well as at the international level. In some missions the main functions may be to create a better economic climate in the host country; in others it may be to conduct fact-finding and make recommendations to the government; in still others it may be to self-educate the Japanese business community, public, or government agencies. Whatever the objective, economic missions have an impact on the attitudes, contacts, and careers of the individual participants.

SIGNIFICANCE OF ECONOMIC MISSIONS

In the conceptual framework of Chapter 1 we rejected the notion of a monolithic Japan, Inc., put aside the business-government duality as an analytical approach, and chose instead to focus on the interests of participating groups and individuals from both business and government. At this point we shall digress momentarily to bring in the business-government duality in terms of their sponsorship of economic missions. Table 5 does not distinguish between business and government sponsorship for economic missions (these data are available in Appendix A), but in considering the overall significance of missions it is worthwhile noting that business sponsorship continued to grow during 1956-68 and after. In 1971 there were no less than thirty economic missions—2.5 per month—dispatched by the business community. According to the Japan Economic Journal, "Their dispatch reflects not only Japan's growing internationalization but stands to supplement the Government's diplomatic efforts from a private basis."[30] Three points can be drawn from this quotation.

First, economic missions are used by the Japanese to supplement their professional diplomacy. We have tried to show in this chapter how this is done, using examples drawn primarily from the Takasugi Mission to Indonesia, a government sponsored mission.

TABLE 5

Economic Missions, 1956-68

Region and Country	Total	1956	1957	1958	1959	1960	1961	1962	1963	1964	1965	1966	1967	1968
Western Europe	20			1		1	1	4	4	3	1	3		2
United Kingdom	(1)							(1)						
Italy	(1)							(1)						
Austria	(1)													(1)
Pacific Basin	15			2	1		3	1		2	2	1	1	2
United States	(9)			(1)	(1)		(1)	(1)		(1)	(1)	(1)	(1)	(1)
Canada	(6)			(1)			(2)	(1)		(1)				(1)
Australia	(3)			(1)			(1)				(1)			
New Zealand	(3)			(1)			(1)				(1)			
Southeast Asia	10	3				1	1	1		2			1	1
Indonesia	(2)	(1)												(1)
Philippines	(1)	(1)												
Burma	(1)					(1)								
Malaysia	(1)						(1)							
East Asia	9	1				2	1	2	1		1	1		
Communist China	(6)	(1)				(2)		(1)	(1)		(1)			
Nationalist China	(1)						(1)							
Korea (ROK)	(2)							(1)			(1)			
Eastern Europe	8							2	1	1	2	1		1
USSR	(5)							(2)			(2)	(1)		
North Africa & Middle East	7					2	1			1	1	1		1
Iran	(2)					(1)								(1)
Africa	7					1	2	1			1	1	1	
Nigeria	(2)					(1)	(1)							
Ghana	(1)					(1)								
South Asia	6						2			1	1	1	1	
Pakistan	(2)						(1)						(1)	
India	(1)											(1)		
Central America & Caribbean	5				1			1			1	1		1
Mexico	(1)													(1)
South America	5								1		2	1		1
Brazil	(1)													(1)
Mediterranean	1					1								
Total	93	4		3	2	8	11	12	7	10	12	11	4	9

Note: Missions to specific countries are listed in parentheses and are also included in regional figures. Missions to more than one region are counted as separate missions. The table includes only government sponsored missions or those sponsored by one or more of the four major business associations, and occasional cosponsorship by the Japan Productivity Center or the Japan Foreign Trade Council. Commercial or trade missions, technical missions, fisheries missions, missions sent by company or trade federation sponsors, and those missions that lack broad support of the big business community are excluded.

Sources: Official reports of missions; Ministry of Foreign Affairs, Waga gaiko no kinkyo [Present state of our foreign relations] (Tokyo: Ministry of Finance, annual); Keizai Doyukai and Keidanren staff interviews and documents, particularly "Kaigi haken keizai shisetsudanra hokokusho tenji mokuroku" [Catalog of reports on overseas economic missions and the like] (Tokyo: Keizai Dantai Rengokai, 1971); Japanese and English language newspapers.

Second, the efficacy of these missions as a supplement depends on all participants abiding by the characteristic Japanese style of cooperative-competition. This is not a fixed cultural trait that can be assumed as a constant. It depends on the presence of an overall interest which participants share, and separate interests by which all participants have something to gain: As long as this holds true, as it did for the Takàsugi example and for 1956-68 in general, participants will work hard on economic missions.

Internationally and domestically, Japanese business and government needed each other's close cooperation through 1968. If each grows sufficiently in strength to achieve its special interests independent of the other (for example, thirty private missions per year), the need to cooperate may be proportionately lessened. As business develops its own institutions for communicating with foreign governments, it may need less help from the Foreign Ministry, just as when business becomes stronger to compete with foreign companies within Japan it will need the protection of MITI proportionately less. The same point could be made in reverse regarding missions to Korea, China, and the Soviet Union, where stronger inter-governmental relations may lead to a proportionate decrease in the need of the Foreign Ministry for business support. The point remains to be tested, but the close cooperation and cosponsorship of business and government on economic missions in 1956-68 does not necessarily hold for the decade of the 1970s and beyond.

The third point has to do with the word "internationalization" in the quotation: If by this is meant that Japan is increasing its economic ties with all nations (by our interpretation so as to avoid dependence on any single nation), then this applies to groups and individuals as well. Even economic missions themselves are becoming internationalized. In October 1968 a team of businessmen from Germany, Japan, the United States, Great Britain, Italy, and France spent six days in Ceylon, at the invitation of the Ceylon government, in discussing conditions for foreign investment in Ceylon.[31] A similar international mission visited Thailand earlier in 1968. If this trend continues, one can expect to find internationalist business leaders joining with their foreign counterparts to put collective pressure on governments, national or international, for legislative reforms or policy changes. This point, and the second point on the growth of business association institutions capable of sustaining their own private economic diplomacy, will be clarified in the next two chapters which deal with diplomatic forms sponsored exclusively by business in cooperation with government.

NOTES

1. Keidanren Geppo, December 1967, pp. 13-14, and Keidanren Review, March 1968, p. 34. This point was made in a Keidanren roundtable discussion by Katsumi Yamagata, chairman of Yamashita Shinnihon Steamship, whose trip in 1951 set a precedent for private economic diplomacy.

2. Ministry of Foreign Affairs, Waga gaiko no kinkyo [Present state of our foreign affairs] (Tokyo: Finance Ministry, 1962), p. 311.

3. Ibid., 1961.

4. "Ho Mareishiya keizai chosadan" [Economic survey team to Malaysia] (Tokyo: Keizai Dantai Rengokai, 1963).

5. "Seifu haken ho Indoneshia keizai shisetsudan hokokusho" [Report of the government sponsored economic mission to Indonesia], hereafter cited as Takasugi Report (Tokyo: Ho Indoneshia Keizai Shisetsudan, 1969).

"Japanese Government Economic Mission to the Republic of Indonesia, September 29-October 9, 1968 "(Tokyo: Ho Indoneshia Keizai Shisetsudan, 1968).

6. The Djakarta Conference of August 1967 was one of an ongoing series of international businessmen's conferences sponsored by Stanford Research Institute. See Yoshizane Iwasa, "Taiheiyo Indoneshia jitsugyojin kaigi ni shusseiki shite" [On attending the Pacific-Indonesia Industrialists Conference], Keidanren Geppo, September 1967; p. 34, and "The Djakarta Report," SRI International, No. 3 (September 1967).

7. Japan Times, November 4, 1968, p. 11.

8. Japan Times, August 17, 1968, p. 11.

9. "Minkan no ugoki kappatsuka" [Increasingly active moves by private interests], Asahi Shimbun, July 2, 1968.

10. As officially stated, "The purpose of this mission, besides deepening the good relations between Indonesia and Japan, was to discuss frankly various fundamental problems of Japan-Indonesia economic cooperation, especially problems of capital investment." Takasugi report, p. 1.

11. During the selection process for a mission to the United States, for example, "Ishizaka had been compelled to enlarge the mission in the face of mounting dissatisfaction by some large business and industrial groups over what they considered a heavy imbalance in the selection of the mission members in favor of only the revived Mitsui financial and industrial group." Japan Times, February 27, 1961, p. 10.

12. Background information on the Takasugi mission not found in the report itself was derived largely from interviews with staff members of the mission and of Keidanren. Responsibility for errors, however, rests solely with the author.

13. Other members included Toyoroku Ando, chairman, Keidanren Committee on Transportation; Seiichiro Hirota, President, Toyo Rayon; Masashi Isano, President, Kawasaki Dockyard; Kenjiro Kawakami, President, Sumitomo Metal Mining; Dr. Koji Kobayashi, President, Nippon Electric; Tadayasu Kodama, Chairman, NYK Line; Dr. Shizuma Matsuo, President, Japan Air Lines; Kiyoshi Uematsu, President, Furukawa Electric; and Rikuzo Koto, Senior Managing Director, Keidanren.

The Takasugi mission ranks as the "largest and most impressive foreign business mission to visit Djakarta since 1945." Lawrence Olson, Japan in Postwar Asia (New York: Praeger, for the Council on Foreign Relations, 1970), p. 191. See also "Seijishoku ga takamaru, zaikai minkan gaiko [Political coloring deepens in private economic diplomacy], Keizai Tembo, October 1, 1968, p. 19.

14. Interview with Yasuo Takeyama, Chief, Editorial Staff, Nihon Keizei Shimbun, February 18, 1969.

15. "Japanese Government Economic Mission to the Republic of Indonesia, September 29-October 9, 1968" (Tokyo: Ho Indonesian Keizai Shisetsudan, 1968), p. 18. The Agriculture and Forestry Ministry is not often represented on economic missions but sent an adviser in this case because of the importance of Indonesian agriculture and extensive timber reserves. Discussions covered rice, timber, dried seaweed (nori), and fertilizer.

16. Interview with Tadayoshi Yamada, Executive Director, Yawata Iron and Steel Co. Yamada accompanied the Inayama mission to Canada in 1964 but intended his remark to apply to missions in general. He was in favor of missions for reasons other than listing policy recommendations.

17. The first recommendation to the Japanese government was to improve its own conditions for channeling investment funds to Indonesia. This has been especially troublesome in obtaining the approval of joint ventures with Indonesian companies. The "time lag" according to Iwasa's press conference statement (Japan Times, October 10, 1968, p. 14), is what turns Indonesian eyes toward American and European firms who can move much faster to get projects started. One might add that this also contributes to the appearance of discrimination against Japanese capital. At any rate, the Takasugi mission placed this matter at the top of its list of recommendations to the Japanese government. In addition to recommendations for study of tax reforms and an investment guarantee system, the proposal recommended the strengthening of the economic section of the Japanese Embassy at Djakarta and the dispatch of Japanese management specialists along with the importation of research students from Indonesia.

18. Takasugi Report, p. 1.

19. Interviews with Akira Saito, political reporter, Mainichi Shimbun, February 24, 1969, and Atuso Ueda, Assistant to the Managing Director, Keidanren, March 13, 1969. For a more pessimistic evaluation of the mission's results ("Its results were uncertain") see Olson, op. cit., p. 191.

20. Japan Times, October 14, 1968, p. 11.

21. Japan Times, October 23, 1968, p. 12. Dr. Okita visited Indonesia the week of October 7 as an economic adviser to the Indonesian government. He is also chairman of the Japan Economic Research Center, an affiliate of the newspaper Nihon Keizai Shimbun.

22. Japan Economic Journal, November 5, 1968, p. 15, and April 20, 1971, p. 3. The trend toward increased Japanese aid to Indonesia has continued. The figures were $150 million in fiscal 1970 and $155 million in fiscal 1971. Of the latter, $125 million was for development projects and commodity aid, repayable over 25 years (including 7 years grace) at three percent interest.

23. Japan Economic Journal, November 5, 1968, p. 12.

24. Ibid., from remarks to the press by Tsunekazu Namba, president of Sanyo Pulp, a member of the Takasugi mission, and not surprisingly, the first chairman of the new Keidanren committee on forestry. He also concluded a timber agreement for a consortium of Japanese companies including Sanyo Pulp. The consortium appears to be an increasingly popular approach for Japanese investment in developing countries.

25. Of interest in this project was the change from production-sharing to an arrangement which allows joint management as well as capital participation. The former agreement under production-sharing with Indonesian management had yielded only approximately 12,000 cubic meters a month over an area of 500,000 hectares. The new agreement opened up eight units of 100,000 hectares each, with a production target of 100,000 cubic meters per year. Authorized capital for each unit was one million dollars with 90 percent supplied by the Japanese. The share-holding ratio was to be changed to 50-50 eight years after the first dividend is paid. Japan Times, October 14, 1968, p. 11.

26. Japan Times, October 15, 1968, p. 8. The agreement called for the export to Indonesia of 890,000 tons of fertilizers for utilization under Indonesia's five-year plan. The agreement itself was for a three-year period beginning in 1969. It coincided nicely with a bumper crop of rice in Indonesia which would allow a switch from the purchase of Japanese rice to fertilizers.

27. Interview with Atsuo Ueda, Assistant to the Managing Director, Keidanren, March 13, 1969.

28. Tokyo Monitor, April 6-19, 1971, p. 8.
29. Keidanren Shuho, No. 910 (April 3, 1969), p. 4.
30. Japan Economic Journal, January 12, 1971, p. 13.
31. Japan Times, October 11, 1968, p. 14.

5

JOINT
ECONOMIC
COMMITTEES

A joint economic committee (<u>keizai godo iinkai</u>) is an international body of businessmen consisting of standing national committees which meet together periodically on a bilateral or multilateral basis. Separate national committees are established in each of two or more countries, for example, the Japan-Soviet Joint Cooperation Committee (Japanese) and the Soviet-Japan Joint Cooperation Committee (Russian). When meeting together they become a joint economic committee which is treated in this study as a single committee rather than two national committees. National committees alternate as the host country for joint meetings which are normally held annually. In Japan, most of the joint economic committees are associated with Keidanren whose extensive committee structure and staff can provide needed secretariat services. This institutional feature, business sponsorship, and the assumption of regularly scheduled meetings distinguish the joint committee from other forms of private economic diplomacy.

The countries with which the Japanese have established joint economic committees (see Table 6) are trading partners of importance or potential importance to the Japanese business community. The Japanese government does not participate directly in joint committee meetings, as it does with economic missions and roving ambassadors, although it may send observers or guest speakers to meetings. It does recognize the joint economic committee form as a useful adjunct to professional diplomacy.[1]

To be more specific about the goals of that diplomacy we will set the tone for this chapter with a quotation from the Japan Economic Journal which refers to Japanese businessmen but could apply to diplomats as well.

What top (Japanese) businessmen fear most at the present time is Japan's isolation in the international world.

TABLE 6

Joint Economic Committee Meetings, 1956-68

Country	Total	1956	1957	1958	1959	1960	1961	1962	1963	1964	1965	1966	1967	1968
Republic of China	14	0	2		2		1	1	1	1	1	1	2	1
Australia	6			1					1	1	1	1	1	1
Pacific Basin (Nissho)	4												1	3
USSR	3											1	1	1
France	3											1	1	1
Italy	3									1	1			1
United States (Doyukai)	2							2						
Argentina	2											1	1	
India (Doyukai)	2												1	1
Total	39	0	2	1	2	0	1	3	2	3	3	5	8	9

Note: Keidanren serves as the chief sponsoring organization for joint economic committees except as noted for Keizai Doyukai, and PBEC, whose secretariat is located at Nissho. Since 1968 joint committees with Germany, Sweden, and Thailand have been added.

Sources: Official reports of joint economic committee meetings; Ministry of Foreign Affairs, Waga gaiko no kinkyo [Present state of our foreign relations] (Tokyo: Ministry of Finance, annual); Keizai Doyukai and Keidanren staff interviews and documents, particularly "Kaigi haken keizai shisetsu-missions and the like (Tokyo: Keizai Dantai Rengokai, 1971); Japanese and English language newspapers.

. . . While businessmen agree that Japan-U.S. ties should constitute the "axis" of their activities, there is a growing sentiment among them that Japan should now modify its past one-sided reliance on the U.S., spread its ties to Communist Bloc countries and particularly EEC for avoiding the possibility of being internationally isolated.[2]

The data of Tables 5 and 6 proved to be consistent with this statement beginning with the late 1960s in that special attention was given to Western Europe and the Soviet Union. We shall also argue here that the rapidly increasing activity centering on the Pacific Basin represents a Japanese attempt to lessen its "one-sided reliance" on the United States although still maintaining, even expanding, its American market. Comparing the economic missions of Table 5 and the joint economic committees of Table 6, we find the frequency of business cooperating with government on economic missions to the above key areas to be rather steady, while the joint economic committees under the exclusive sponsorship of business shows rapid growth beginning in 1966. This chapter will examine this growth of business institutions at the joint committee level, again in terms of underlying interests.

Individual participation in any of the joint economic committees enhances the Japanese business leader's standing among his peers but Shigeo Nagano's leadership role in those for Australia, the Pacific Basin, USSR, and India suggests how small is the group at the top of Japan's private economic diplomacy. Representative of this group, Nagano has been characterized as an internationalist business leader because wherever he goes he seems to form joint committee and business conferences.[3]

Among the joint economic committees formed since 1957 we shall pay particular attention to two in which Nagano played a leading role: the Pacific Basin Economic Council (PBEC), and the Japan-Soviet Joint Cooperation Committee.

As chairman of the largest steel company in the world, Nagano's participation reflected Japan's priority for expanding Asian-Pacific trade and securing stable sources of raw materials—major agenda topics of both joint committees. The Japan-Soviet committee was aimed at a single nearby area as a potential large supplier of raw materials; PBEC was a multilateral initiative to combine and balance the same Japanese interests with four other Pacific powers as equals: Australia, New Zealand, Canada, and the United States.

THE PACIFIC BASIN ECONOMIC COUNCIL (PBEC)

PBEC* consists of business leaders from five industrialized Pacific states organized to promote economic collaboration among member countries and to cooperate with the less developed countries.[4] Structurally, power resides in five national committees. Each has one vote at meetings and all decisions are by unanimous vote. Each national committee elects its own chairman who also serves on the steering committee which sets up the agenda for each general meeting.† The PBEC president presides at steering committee and general meetings but his power depends on the support of each of the other four national committee chairmen.

The national committees are affiliated with major business associations in their respective countries. As of 1968 there were eleven affiliated associations‡ of which Nissho was the only one for Japan. The associations represent bases of support and legitimacy for each national committee and also a base for secretariat services

---

*The original English name of Pacific Basin Economic Cooperation Committee was changed to Pacific Basin Economic Cooperation Council at the Second General Meeting, San Francisco, May 1969. The word "cooperation" was dropped at the Fourth General Meeting, Vancouver, May 1971.

†For example, respresentatives to the first meeting of the steering committee in Honolulu, February 1968, included: Sir Edward Warren, The Wallarah Coal Company Ltd. (Australia); R. G. Speirs, R. G. Speirs Ltd. (New Zealand); A. Olaf Wolff, Microsystems International Ltd. (Canada); Ransom M. Cook, Wells Fargo Bank (U.S.A.); and Shigeo Nagano, Fuji Iron and Steel Ltd. (Japan). All were chairmen of their respective national committees. Also present from Japan were Yoshizane Iwasa and Eiji Kageyama, Secretary General for the Japan National Committee of PBEC and managing director of Nissho.

‡Associated Chambers of Manufacturers of Australia; Canadian Chamber of Commerce; Canadian Manufacturers Association; Japan Chamber of Commerce and Industry (Nissho); Associated Chambers of Commerce of New Zealand; Federated Farmers of New Zealand; New Zealand Bankers Association; New Zealand Manufacturers Federation; United States Council, International Chamber of Commerce; National Association of Manufacturers; United States Chamber of Commerce. In addition, Stanford Research Institute provides research and secretariat support, especially for the U.S. National Committee of PBEC. SRI International, No. 6 (1968).

if needed. They also act as sources for nominations of individual businessmen to be invited, for attendance at PBEC meetings is by invitation only. Americans who attended the first general meeting were nominated by the U.S. Council of the International Chamber of Commerce, the U.S. Chamber of Commerce, and the National Association of Manufacturers. However, invitations are issued by the secretariat of each national committee, not by the affiliated business associations.

For funding purposes, membership in a national committee is by company, and meeting costs are billed to each member company by the national committee on a pro rata basis. But attendance is generally limited to senior or executive vice-presidents and up.

The above structure notwithstanding, PBEC is an organization of individual business leaders.[5] They are conscious of performing a supplementary role to their country's multilateral economic diplomacy but they do not represent their government or its official policy. They vote on the basis of their country's business interests but they speak as individual executives of specific companies and industries. And the delegation lists are really determined by which business leaders take a personal interest in the purpose, scope, membership, and activities of PBEC. In each national committee, one or two individuals were chiefly responsible for PBEC's existence. For Japan that man was Shigeo Nagano whose role in PBEC was central, before and after its birth as an organization.

The Japanese claim to have originated and developed the idea for an organization like PBEC[6] although the Australians first proposed it formally in 1963 at the first meeting of another joint economic committee, the Japan-Australia Business Cooperation Committee.[7] This Japan-Australia committee had been proposed earlier by Nagano when he was chairman of a Nissho sponsored economic mission to Australia in March 1961.[8] When regular meetings of the Japan-Australia Committee began in 1963 the same familiar faces appeared: Adachi as Japanese chairman, Nagano and Uemura as vice-chairmen, with the remaining members drawn from Keidanren, Nissho, and the Japan Foreign Trade Council.

After exploratory discussions in the Japan-Australia Committee, and initial communication with business circles in New Zealand, the United States, and Canada, PBEC began its official existence at an organizational meeting in Tokyo, April 1967, directly following the Fifth Japan-Australia Committee meeting.[9] Nagano was elected the first chairman of the new organization (Taiheiyo Keizai Iinkai), but his first task was a sales job for at that point only Japan and Australia were officially members. New Zealand had sent observers but American and Canadian business leaders had only expressed interest without commiting themselves.

Nagano paid a visit to North America to gain support for PBEC and found some apathy there, particularly from East Coast businessmen. They were reluctant to participate if it might appear that they were official representatives of the United States. He solved the problem through support from colleagues, particularly Iwasa who set up meetings for Nagano with West Coast businessmen who in turn helped Nagano convince East Coast businessmen.[10] He also received general support from Kikawada who backed the idea of a Pacific Community through his chairmanship of an economic mission to the Midwest in 1967.[11] As a result of these efforts American and Canadian business circles agreed to participate in time to make PBEC a five-nation organization at its first general meeting at Sydney in 1968.[12] It constituted "the first time for the five Pacific nations to hold a formal get-together on issues in the Asia-Pacific area irrespective of its government or private character."[13] A PBEC general meeting typically occupies up to 100 business leaders for over three days. There will be a reception to start off officially, but this will have been preceded by a steering committee meeting, press conference, and informal caucuses by national committees to coordinate their positions. After opening speeches at the first plenary session, the bulk of the work begins at meetings of the standing committees: tourism, transportation, human resources, natural resources, and economic development. Additional plenary sessions are devoted to national economic projections, guest speakers, and special problems such as membership. Final summations, press conference, and banquet close the meeting.

Work in the standing committees takes the form of reviewing the working papers in the respective fields, with discussion aimed first at understanding the position of each of the five national committees on an issue, then to move toward a recommendation for the final plenary session at which the chairman of each standing committee reports on the findings of his committee.

The substantive work for the standing committee deliberations is done in advance through working papers by particular delegates interested in a topic or project. These are mineographed or printed along with delegate rosters and photographs by each national committee. If a paper proposes specific action, such as a management training program for developing Pacific states, it will undergo discussion, modification, be dropped, or be recommended to the plenary session. But the meetings through 1968 were content to work out procedures and priorities for PBEC itself. This apparent lack of action projects had to do with inherent structural limitations.

PBEC is an organization to promote the interests of private enterprise; interests which are compatible with but not identical to the interests of their respective governments. As described by

Ransom Cook, former chairman of the U.S. National Committee and of Wells Fargo Bank, the national committee has the blessing of its government but no participation or tangible support. Delegates attend as private businessmen. This limits the diplomatic value of PBEC to the mutual exchange of unofficial policy and information.

Furthermore PBEC membership is limited to private enterprise of five industrialized states only, despite its dual purpose of helping the developed and the developing—to strengthen economic relationships among the five member nations and to stimulate international business opportunities in the developing nations of the Pacific Basin. Business executives from Taiwan, Korea, and South Vietnam requested observer status in 1968, and the Philippines, Thailand, Indonesia, and Fiji expressed interest, but businessmen from the five member countries remained divided on the issue. PBEC is, after all, a rich man's club by reason of its membership, despite denials by Nagano.[14] Ultimately it must be judged on how well it fulfills both parts of its dual purpose, the developed and the developing.

Lack of a permanent secretariat, not a problem for a bilateral joint economic committee but a problem for a five sided organization, was dealt with by rotating the secretariat with the office of the president. Nagano remained as president from 1967 to 1970 for which period the secretariat for both PBEC and the Japan National Committee also remained at Nissho, specifically with the managing director, Eiji Kageyama. A permanent secretariat was discussed but not approved because of a lack of funds—PBEC has no funds of its own—and because of a fear that PBEC would thereby lose its flexible, decentralized quality as an organization. No national committee wanted to give up its autonomy for the sake of more action and central coordination.

Of the action projects initiated through 1968, the only one to become operational was the Private Investment Corporation for Asia (PICA), a transnational corporation which was organized with the support of PBEC and other organizations, to provide loans and management consulting to private enterprise in the developing countries of Asia.[15] It parallels the Asian Development Bank but deals with private enterprise rather than governments. In its transnational mix of stockholders and management it was modeled after the Atlantic Community Development Group for Latin America (ADELA). PICA opened its offices in Tokyo in 1969 with approximately 120 participating firms and $16.8 million in paid-in capital divided in thirds among the United States, Japan, and investing firms from Australia, Canada, and Europe.[16] PICA is of interest here as an offshoot of PBEC because, like PBEC, it provides a multilateral mechanism for Japan to avoid being isolated between developed Pacific states, on the one hand, and developing Asian states, on the other. Given the mounting resistence to Japanese capital investment in Southeast Asia, PICA represents a means for the Japanese to invest on equal terms in a multilateral context with proportionately less political disadvantages and less financial risk.

The Japanese government participates in neither PBEC nor PICA, although it welcomes both. Participants are the real gainers in private economic diplomacy, and the Japanese government stands to gain only indirectly. In the multilateral setting of PBEC, Japan enjoys a more comfortable feeling of near equality—the status of a major power though not a super-power. At the same time, it can freely build its relationships among other industrialized Pacific powers. An American delegate wryly mixed his metaphors when he remarked that Japan was in PBEC to get its teeth more firmly into Australian iron ore and coal; Australia was in it to get the Americans to help get Japan off Australia's back, and so on.

Neither business nor government intended PBEC to develop into an EEC of the Pacific. Political ties or even a common tariff were not contemplated. Taizo Ishizaka had to reassure the British on this point by means of an economic mission to the United Kingdom in 1967, for the British feared further weakening of the Commonwealth. Nagano and Iwasa were careful in public statements to avoid comparison of PBEC with the EEC. Instead they called attention to PBEC's nongovernmental character by which EEC-type measures were virtually impossible. Nevertheless, the degree of interdependence was high in terms of percentage of intragroup trade to total national trade. As of 1968 Japan ranked in the middle in order of dependence: New Zealand, 36 percent; United States, 37 percent; Japan, 38 percent; Australia, 40 percent; and Canada, 73 percent.[17]

Business interests in PBEC stood to advance, and be advanced by, concurrent trade and joint venture projects among member companies. In Nagano's area of interest, raw materials for the steel industry, several Japanese steel, chemical, and trading companies joined with Kaiser Steel and Kaiser Aluminum in a joint development venture in Australia. Discussions at PBEC accelerated this cooperation and PBEC was accelerated by it.[18] Later, the successor to Ransom Cook as chairman of the American national committee was C. W. Robinson, president of Marcona Corporation, a leading shipper of iron ore and other raw materials. Unless these interests continue to support each other, it is doubtful that PBEC will continue to be viable.

When asked about the value of PBEC, the president of an American oil company replied that it is to gain personal perspective and recognize individual differences, to establish personal contact on which joint ventures and other actions can be taken. This can be said of all joint economic committees, perhaps even more so when it comes to dealing with the Soviet Union.

THE JAPAN-SOVIET
JOINT COOPERATION COMMITTEE

The Japan-Soviet Joint Cooperation Committee (heareafter
abbreviated as Joint Committee) serves to establish and maintain a
favorable atmosphere for trade and investment as do other joint committees, economic missions, and roving ambassadors, but it differs
in that the negotiation of agreements—especially the joint development
of Siberia—was a primary purpose from the very first meeting of
the Joint Committee in 1966.

The Japan side of the committee is headquartered and staffed
at Keidanren, with a membership made up of executives from Keidanren member firms who have business interests in the Soviet Union.
As with economic missions, the chairman (Adachi to 1968) selects
members after consultation with Keidanren leaders and government
circles.

Because the committee does conclude agreements on a project
basis it requires unusually close coordination with the government,
especially Foreign Ministry negotiations of trade agreements on a
five year and annual quota basis. To analyze the structure and operation of the Joint Committee in the context of its relations with Soviet
and Japanese governments we shall review the step by step role each
played in the first agreement concluded under the Joint Committee,
the timber agreement of July 29, 1968.[19]

The key Japanese government official in this agreement was
the Director of the Economic Affairs Bureau in the Foreign Ministry.
He (or at the administrative level his chief of the East-West Trade
Division) represented the Japanese government in negotiations with
the Soviet government and in liaison with the Joint Committee. After
the 1966-70 Japan-Soviet Trade Agreement was concluded in January
1966, it was his job to negotiate annual agreements, based on the
five year agreement, with his Soviet counterpart, the Soviet Trade
Representative in Japan. Through detailed negotiations they would
readjust annual product lists, quantities, and amounts. In 1968 this
was concluded between K. Tsurumi, Director of the Economic Affairs
Bureau, and V. B. Spandaryan, the Soviet Trade Representative.[20]

Meanwhile, the Joint Committee had been discussing development of Siberia at its meetings of March 1966 in Tokyo, and the
second meeting of June 1967 in Moscow.[21] The Soviet side of the
committee consists of representatives from the All-Soviet Union
Commercial Council. After initial discussions the two sides found
a need to establish subcommittees, or committees of experts, to
negotiate details for each major project proposed. These were the
equivalent of a commercial mission following up an economic mission.
If one subcommittee could reach agreement then its project could

move to the next level down, the company level where it would be carried out.

Forestry was one of the expert committees formed at the second meeting of the Joint Committee in 1967. Although MITI and some business leaders still had reservations, Yoshinari Kawai did not and he was made chairman of the experts committee on forestry.[22] It was Kawai, former chairman of Komatsu Manufacturing, who had led a trade mission to the Soviet Union in August 1962 at which time he proposed to Khrushchev his idea for joint development of Siberia.[23] This Kawai Proposal gradually took on substantive content and became known as the Kawai Plan.[24]

At each stage of the negotiations, the lumber committee would of course consult not only the Economic Affairs Bureau, but the Ministry of Agriculture and Forestry, MITI, Finance Ministry, Keidanren officials, Japan Paper and Pulp Association, and colleagues in the lumber industry and trading companies. On July 23, 1968, while the negotiations were still going on, Kawai set up a new company, K. S. Industry Company, which included Komatsu and thirteen other Japanese manufacturing and trading firms.

Finally, on July 29, Kawai signed a lumber import agreement for 1969-73 with V. N. Akkuratov, his counterpart and president of the Soviet Lumber Product Export Corporation.[25] On the contract, Akkuratov represented the All-Soviet Foreign Trade Corporation EXPORTRES as party to the contract and Kawai represented K-S Industry as the other party. Additional Japanese companies involved were named in the contract but it stipulated that K. S. Industry was responsible for all companies to abide by the terms.

The project then had to move back to the government side where on August 15, Foreign Minister Takeo Miki and Soviet Foreign Trade Minister Nikolai S. Patolichev exchanged protocol letters formalizing the agreement.

K. S. Sangyo could then go to work, and general discussions resumed at the third meeting of the Joint Committee, December 9-11, in Tokyo.[26] The mimeographed list of participants at this meeting named sixty-four Japanese delegates, about twice the number of joint economic committee meetings abroad, and with a preponderance of trading companies represented. Some of the customary names appeared—Uemura, Nagano, Anzai—but some of the more free enterprise oriented names were absent—Ishizaka, Kikawada, and Iwasa. No Japanese government officials attended, although the Soviet side included V. B. Spandaryan who wears government and business hats in contrast to the separate roles on the Japanese side.

The above structure appears cumbersome, and the flow of negotiation circular, but it is the natural product of a centrally planned economy negotiating large scale contracts with a cooperative-competitive free enterprise economy. If similar agreements are concluded in the areas of gas, coal, copper, and oil, they will have undergone the same process: government trade agreement, committee general discussion, expert subcommitee negotiation, company contract, government endorsement. The Japan-Soviet Joint Cooperation Committee is unique in this respect but our picture of private economic diplomacy would not be complete without it.

In addition to procedural problems, there were serious substantive problems, despite "an evolutionary change in Japan-Soviet trade relations" and "an entirely new stage" lauded by Soviet Foreign Trade Minister Patolichev on the occasion of signing the Siberian timber agreement.[27] First of all, the scale of joint Siberian development envisaged by the Soviets, according to economist Saburo Okita, requires capital beyond Japanese means.[28] Second, a serious and continuing trade imbalance developed in favor of the Soviet Union (see Table 7).[29] The communique ending the 1968 joint committee meeting called for further efforts to achieve an expansion of trade between the two countries on a balanced basis.[30] Not the least of the basic problems is a difference in geographic interests: Exactly what territory should Siberia include? The Soviets would like it to mean Soviet Central Asia to the Ural Mountains. The Japanese prefer it to include only Far Eastern Siberia. They use the word en-kaishu, or Maritime Province, which overlaps but differs from the Soviet concept embracing proposals for Western Siberia.[31] Such terms differ because the economic objectives of the two countries differ. The Japanese goal is profit and access to raw materials and markets; the Soviet goal is the development of Siberia in the long range national interest, preferably by repayment to Japan in the form of goods produced and at prices negotiated without necessarily conforming to minimum profit margins or world price standards. In Shigeo Nagano's view, "Real possibilities of trade are being ruined because of the difficulty of reconciling Soviet-Japanese requirements within the narrow confines of the state trading corporation system."[32]

Economic differences notwithstanding, the Sato administration had sound political reasons for its enthusiasm over economic cooperation with the Soviets.[33] Favorable indications include the probable opening of a JETRO office in Moscow in exchange for a Soviet trade office in Osaka, and progress in negotiations toward developing the Tyumen oil fields in Western Siberia.[34] Premier Sato would have liked to use Japanese-Soviet economic diplomacy, including joint economic committee negotiations, as a lever to advance Japan's foreign policy goals vis-a-vis the Soviet Union. Foremost of these goals was the return to Japan of the northern islands—Habomai, Shikotan, Etorofu, and Kunashiri—and conclusion of a Japan-Soviet

TABLE 7

Japan's Trade with the USSR, 1956-68
(thousands of dollars)

Calendar Year	Exports	Imports	Both Ways	Balance
1956	760	2,869	3,629	-2,109
1957	9,295	12,326	21,621	-3,031
1958	18,103	22,168	40,271	-4,065
1959	23,027	39,491	62,518	-16,464
1960	59,976	87,025	147,001	-27,049
1961	65,380	145,409	210,789	-480,029
1962	149,390	147,309	296,699	+2,081
1963	158,136	161,940	320,076	-3,804
1964	181,811	226,729	408,540	-44,918
1965	168,358	240,198	408,556	-71,840
1966	214,022	300,361	514,383	-86,339
1967	157,688	453,918	611,606	-296,230
1968	179,018	463,512	642,530	-284,494

Sources: Tsusho Sangyosho (MITI) Tsusho hakusho [Foreign trade white paper], 1958, pp. 319-20 and 1961, p. 529. Okurasho Kanzeikyoku hen (Ministry of Finance Customs Bureau, ed.), Gaikoken boeki gaikyo [Summary of Foreign trade], No. 6 (June 1969), p. 56.

peace treaty. When Soviet Foreign Trade Minister Patolichev came to Tokyo to sign the Siberian timber agreement, Premier Sato remarked that the absence of a peace treaty between the two countries might be hampering the expansion of Soviet-Japanese trade.[35] Again, when Soviet Deputy Premier Baybakov visited Tokyo to attend the Japan-Soviet Economic Committee meetings he was pressed, albeit unsuccessfully, on the territorial issue by Premier Sato and Foreign Minister Miki.[36] Thus far these Japanese tactics have not achieved their political goals, but it is instructive to note how private economic diplomacy provides some leverage for them.

As bilateral talks and joint development projects gradually build economic ties, further progress toward a peace treaty and territorial settlements is encouraged, or if not, the Japanese will at least have a potential lever with which to exploit Sino-Soviet or U.S.-Soviet rivalries. There is no evidence that the latter would be allowed to endanger U.S.-Japanese security agreements, however.

Nor would U.S.-Japanese trade be diminished in absolute terms. The Japanese would merely gain from Soviet trade a backstop or bargaining counter against protectionist demands among American business circles.

It is interesting to compare Japanese purposes in the Soviet case as seen through the Joint Committee with those in the Indonesian case as shown in the Takasugi mission (Chapter 3). In both, Japan has shown great eagerness but with a different time perspective. In Indonesia the Japanese are working hard because they are behind time in an area of surging international competition. In Siberia the Japanese are working hard to be prepared ahead of time for the day when Soviet terms will be more realistic, when Japan's capitalization and economic base will be ready for development projects of the huge scale required in Siberia, and when cold war alignments will have eased enough to bring U.S.-Japanese trade into a more reasonable balance with that of Japan's more immediate neighbors to the west and northwest.

The focal point in this effort is the Japan-Soviet Joint Cooperation Committee. This committee and other initiatives of private economic diplomacy have established a rapport with the Soviet Union at a high level, including the premier. According to Saburo Okita this is especially important in Soviet relations because the higher the level of bureaucrat the broader the individual outlook and authority, hence the more that can be accomplished.[37]

Whatever has been accomplished beyond the establishment of a favorable rapport, the benefits to company interests have been slow in coming and less than expected. Although overall Japan-Soviet trade increased more than thirty times from 1957 to 1968 (Table 7), eleven major trading companies participating in the timber agreement found it necessary to cable a request to the Soviet Lumber and Lumber Product Export Corporation to allow cutbacks in Japanese imports of Soviet logs due to excessive shipments contrary to previous agreement. The trading companies even threatened to halt all Japanese ship transport of such Russian supplies.[38]

Among Japanese individuals who benefited, Shigeo Nagano became the leading business figure in Japan-Soviet private economic diplomacy, including three trips to the Soviet Union: As Roving Ambassador in September 1958, as head of a steel industry mission in June 1965, and as head of the Japanese delegation to the second meeting of the Joint Committee in June 1967.[39] The first trip did nothing but plant the seeds for future cooperation. For the second trip he was asked by Ishizaka and Adachi to respond favorably to a proposal by M. V. Nesterov, Chairman of the USSR Chamber of Commerce, to establish a joint chamber of commerce. The Japanese decided to have Nagano counter with a proposal along the lines of the Japan-Australia Business

Cooperation Committee. This was accepted during the steel mission and Nagano signed an agreement which launched the Japan-Soviet Joint Cooperation Committee. His third trip was as delegation leader of the Committee; a delegation of thirty-one committee members in a party of fifty people which included one observer each from the Foreign Ministry, MITI, and the Finance Ministry. It was Nagano's observations on this trip that led to Fuji Iron and Steel's purchase of patents covering a process for operating blast furnaces under high pressures. This meeting also established the subcommittee of experts which led to the timber agreement the following year.

One cannot say that Nagano made a career of Japan-Soviet relations; rather he managed several careers—Australia, Pacific Basin, USSR, India—all related to his stature as an internationalist business leader and to the iron and steel interests of his company. Nagano is also an ardent proponent of the return of the northern islands to Japan, and likes to relate how he found a very old song which includes the islands as Japanese territory.

It is clear, however, that expectations at the first meeting of the Joint Committee in 1966 were premature, for under prevailing world conditions the chances of achieving Japan's political objectives through joint Siberian development were not good, and economically, the Soviets have yet to offer their raw materials on attractive terms. But the thrust of improving Japanese-Soviet relations must be considered on the premise that he who is premature is not likely to be late. The Committee's primary role must be seen as working to establish a favorable climate in which incremental steps can be taken over a period of time. The payoff may be delayed, for example, as long as from the visit of Roving Ambassador Nagano in 1958 to the timber agreement of 1968. More rapid results with the Soviet Union were not to be expected.

SIGNIFICANCE OF JOINT ECONOMIC COMMITTEES

Joint economic committees are the initiative of the business community and by 1966-68 had begun a pattern of considerable institution-building. Table 6 represents only the beginning of a growing list of Japanese business initiatives to discuss general problems with counterparts around the world. The benefactors of all this activity include: (1) The government, particularly the Foreign Ministry, that gains a supplementary channel for two way information to foreign governments; (2) the business community, which acquires a congenial forum where it can pursue its search for raw materials, markets, and joint venture partners, all without depending on the leadership and assistance of government; (3) the individual business leader who by taking on the responsibility for a joint economic committee places himself in a position of centrality in that bilateral economic relationship, thereby increasing his stature with his business association, company, and business leader colleagues.

In providing the government with a supplementary channel—from government to business, to foreign business, to foreign government—the business community does not act like a passive conductor of signals. While it does not make foreign policy it can certainly influence the tempo and direction in which foreign policy is moving. PBEC was a first for business, a move toward regional cooperation ahead of government but with the support of Premier Sato and Foreign Minister Miki.[40] Kiichiro Sato (no relation), chairman of Mitsui Bank, cites PBEC as an example of business taking steps ahead of government, thereby building a foundation for government to use.[41]

This was also true of joint development of Siberia. Although the political objectives have not been gained, and the returns to participating companies have been disappointing, it was another case in which business circles (especially trading firms) were putting pressure on the Japanese government to move, using the joint economic committee as a party to the negotiations.[42] The Soviet situation is unique and Japan must treat each country or region with the appropriate mix of economic missions, roving ambassadors, joint economic committees, and conferences.

Such was the range of Japan's pragmatic private economic diplomacy for 1965-68. As Sebald and Spinks put it, rather prophetically for 1967, Japan is cautiously attempting to develop a broader and more positive Asian-Pacific orientation. "Conceivably, such a broader orientation could include Communist China and possibly the Soviet Union because of expanded trade with Siberia."[43] Recent developments, notably the sudden change in Sino-American relations followed by Japan's recognition of the People's Republic of China, suggest an acceleration toward a more widely cooperative, more independent Japan. By the late 1960s we had already begun to see a Japanese business community begin to build its own institutions and channels of communication, still in cooperation with the Japanese government but gradually less dependent on it.

NOTES

1. Since 1965 the Japanese Foreign Ministry has listed joint economic committees in its annual Diplomatic Blue Book: Ministry of Foreign Affairs, Waga gaiko no kinkyo [Present state of our foreign affairs] (Tokyo: Ministry of Finance).

2. "Business Leaders are Moving to Attain Closer Ties with Europe," Japan Economic Journal, October 26, 1971, p. 2.

3. Hideo Akimoto, Keidanren (Tokyo: Sekkasha, 1968), p. 211.

4. Covenant of the Pacific Basin Economic Council, Article II. Cooperation among members and developing countries are intended to receive equal weight. Interview with Shigeo Nagano, president of Fuji Iron and Steel, March 4, 1969.

5. Early and explicitly Japan made known the high priority it assigned to personal contact through PBEC.

> There is great significance in providing, through the
> medium of the PBEC organization, an opportunity for
> the business leaders of the five countries to get together
> and state their opinions and positions concerning problems
> of the international liquidity, of the introduction of capi-
> tal, of the tariff barrier, of the foreign trade, etc. It is,
> therefore, deemed important that the general meeting
> give ever increasing weight to this aspect of the PBEC
> functions.

Unpublished paper by the Japanese National Committee submitted for consideration by the steering committee meeting of September 23-24, 1968.

6. "Asia-Pacific Economic Sphere: A Step Toward Realization," Asia Scene, March 1968, p. 10. This article credits Nagano with originating the idea for PBEC.

7. Reports are published in Tokyo by the Japan-Australia Committee (Keidanren) for each joint meeting. See, for example, "Dai 5 kai Nichi-Go keizai godo iinkai kaigi kiroku" [Record of the 5th conference of the Japan-Australia joint economic committee] (Tokyo: Nichi-Go Keizai Iinkai, October 1967). For a review of the committee's achievements see R. W. C. Anderson, "Australia-Japan Economic Relations," Pacific Community, January 1970, pp. 303-17.

8. Japan Times, May 18, 1970, p. 11.

9. "Taiheiyo keizai iinkai kaigi kiroku—setsuritsu kaigi" [Record of the founding conference, Pacific Basin Economic Council] (Tokyo: Taiheiyo Keizai Iinkai, October 1967).

10. Interview with Masahisa Segawa, Secretary to the President, The Fuji Bank Ltd., October 26, 1968.

11. Address by Kazutaka Kikawada at a luncheon given for the mission by the U.S.-Japan Trade Council at the Mayflower Hotel in Washington, D.C., June 30, 1967.

12. "Record of the First General Meeting of the Pacific Basin Economic Co-operation Committee," published informally by PBEC,

that is, the national committee of the current president (Japan in 1968) because overall PBEC secretariat responsibilities rotate with the office of president. See also "Sydney Meeting, Pacific Basin Committee, A Report on the First General Meeting—May 9-19, 1968," SRI International, No. 6 (1968).

13. Japan Economic Journal, April 30, 1968, p. 14.

14. Japan Times, August 29, 1968, p. 8.

15. PICA was first proposed formally by the Japanese delegation to the 1968 PBEC meeting at Sydney. Japan Times, February 9, 1969, p. 10, and February 20, 1969, p. 12.

16. The American directors represent First National City, Chase Manhattan, Bank of America, Standard Oil of New Jersey, IBM World Trade Corp., and Wall Street investment houses Lazard Freres and Kuhn, Loeb. The Japanese directors represent—as do most groups involved in private economic diplomacy—a cross-section of banks, trading companies, and internationalist firms: Mitsubishi Trading, Mitsui Trading, Sumitomo Chemical, Nippon Steel, Fuji Bank, Bank of Tokyo, and Nissan Motors. From these firms three individuals are chosen from each of the three national groups to serve on the executive committee. First selected from the American group were Emilio Collada, Standard Oil of New Jersey; Stanley Osborne, Lazard Freres; and Rudolph Peterson, Bank of America. The Japanese contingent consisted of the ever present Iwasa and Nagano, and Sumio Hara, Chairman of the Bank of Tokyo. Osborne chaired the executive committee, Iwasa the board of directors, and the first president was Dr. William A. van Ravesteijn of the Netherlands. "PICA: Private Investment Company for Asia" (general information brochure), April 1969, pp. 9-10.

17. "Record of the First General Meeting of the Pacific Basin Economic Co-operation Committee," p. 32.

18. Interview with Masahisa Segawa, Secretary to the President, The Fuji Bank Ltd., February 21, 1969.

19. A second agreement was concluded in 1970 for the redevelopment of ports and harbor facilities in Vrangel, near Nakhodka. Japan's Export-Import Bank was asked to loan $80 million for Japanese materials and equipment to carry 12 percent annual interest for the first seven years and 6 percent thereafter. Facilities are planned for handling 10 million tons of coal, 800,000 tons of wood chips, and 120,000-140,000 containers annually. Japan Economic Journal, September 29, 1970, p. 12, and March 2, 1971, p. 18.

Still under negotiation within the Joint Committee in 1972, and hence not yet achievements for private economic diplomacy, were: (1) natural gas pipelines from Yakutsk, Siberia, and Ohka, Sakhalin (Japan Economic Journal, October 6, 1970), p. 1; (2) coal at Yakutsk (ibid., October 15, 1968), p. 1; (3) copper at Udokan, Siberia (New

York Times, April 22, 1967); (4) oil from the Tyumen fields, Western Siberia (Japan Economic Journal, June 15, 1971), p. 11.

20. The agreement called for $322 million in Japanese exports and $305 million in imports from the Soviet Union, or a two way trade of $627 million (FOB, payments basis) for calendar 1968. Actual imports were considerably higher (Table 7). For terms of the agreement see Nihon Keizai Shimbun, April 4, 1968.

21. Japan Quarterly, Vol. 13 (1966), p. 405, and "Nichiso-Sonichi keizai iinkai dainikai godoiinkai hokokusho" [Report of the second joint committee meeting of the Japan-USSR and USSR-Japan economic committees] (Tokyo: Nichiso Keizai Iinkai, November 1967).

22. For Kawai's perspective see Yoshinari Kawai, "Japanese-Soviet Cooperation for Development of Siberia," Japan's Industrial Role (Tokyo: Asahi Evening News, 1968), p. 20. For Yuzo Arai's September 1966 mission to Siberia and Moscow, see "Shiberia-Kyokuto Kaihatsu to Nichi-So keizai koryu: Seifu haken dainiji keizai shisetsudan hokoku" [Siberia-Far East development and Japan-Soviet economic exchange: report of the second government sponsored economic mission] (Tokyo: Keizai Dantai Rengokai, 1967).

23. Japan Times, July 30, 1968, p. 9. There were also two government sponsored economic missions which improved rapport and developed the idea of joint development in Siberia. For Kogoro Uemura's August 1965 discussions with Khrushchev as head of the first government sponsored economic mission to the Soviet Union, see "Seifu haken ho So keizai shisetsudan hokokusho" [Report of the government economic mission to the USSR] (Tokyo: Keizai Dantai Rengokai, July 1966).

24. The terms of the timber agreement call for Japanese shipments of $163 million in equipment and workers' consumer goods over a five-year period in return for Siberian timber, paper, and pulp. This is a modest sum compared to other proposed projects which may be one reason it was signed first. Japan Economic Journal, August 6, 1968, p. 1.

25. For the full text of the agreement see Nikkan Ajiya Boeki, August 2, 1968.

26. Keidanren Shuho, No. 896 (December 19, 1968), pp. 5-8.

27. Japan Times, August 16, 1968, p. 9.

28. Saburo Okita, Nihon keizai no bijion [A vision of the Japanese economy] (Tokyo: Daimondosha, 1968), pp. 212, 215.

29. For Siberian developments to 1968 and trade imbalance as a limiting factor, see "Present and Future Outlook of Russo-Japanese Trade Ties," Asahi Evening News, May 21, 1968, p. 6. Trade deficits for 1969 and 1970 were reduced to $193 million and $140 million, respectively. Ministry of International Trade and Industry,

Tsusho hakusho [Foreign trade white paper], 1971, kakuron, pp. 708, 710.

30. Japan Economic Journal, December 17, 1968, p. 1.

31. Okita, op. cit., p. 214.

32. Shigeo Nagano, "Russo-Japanese Trade," Japan Quarterly, 14 (October-December 1967): p. 425.

33. Japan Economic Journal, August 10, 1971, p. 1.

34. Ibid., June 15, 1971.

35. Japan Times, August 16, 1968, p. 1, and Asahi Shimbun, August 16, 1968, p. 1.

36. Interview with John M. Gregory, Second Secretary, Economic Section, U.S. Embassy, September 12, 1968.

37. Interview with Saburo Okita, President, Japan Economic Research Center, February 17, 1969.

38. Japan Economic Journal, June 1, 1971, p. 12.

39. Nagano, "Russo-Japanese Trade," op. cit., pp. 422-28.

40. Japan Economic Journal, October 29, 1968, p. 2, and an address by Kazutaka Kikawada at a luncheon given by the U.S.-Japan Trade Council at the Mayflower Hotel, Washington, D.C., June 30, 1967.

41. Kiichiro Sato et al., "Minkan keizai gaiko no yakuwari to seika" [The role and results of private economic diplomacy], Keidanren Geppo, December 1967, p. 10.

42. Interview with Saburo Okita, President, Japan Economic Research Center, February 17, 1969.

43. William J. Sebald and C. Nelson Spinks, Japan: Prospects, Options, and Opportunities (Washington, D.C.: American Enterprise Institute for Public Policy Research, 1967), p. 81.

6

International businessmen's conferences (<u>zaikaijin kaigi</u> or <u>jitsugyojin kaigi</u>) are essentially the same as joint economic committees except that they do not necessarily meet regularly and do not maintain a standing staff as do the joint economic committees. Also, conferences tend to be less formal than joint committees, with more emphasis on a free exchange of views among individual businessmen in a cordial atmosphere. Within such an atmosphere they attempt an unofficial exploration and clarification of bilateral or multilateral problems as a supplement to governmental approaches to those problems.

International businessmen's conferences have no official status although they may invite government officials as guests, and their leaders may be in close communication with government circles. They may or may not issue a joint communique and written report after meetings. It is not considered necessary to take action, pass resolutions, or even come to a consensus. The object is to discuss bilateral problems as concerned individuals, thus the conference form is more characteristic of Doyukai than Keidanren or Nissho, although all three participate.

This chapter will focus on several of the Japanese conference associations that deal with the United States, with emphasis on the leadership of Yoshizane Iwasa, in order to show the strengths and weaknesses of the conference form of private economic diplomacy and how they relate to the identity and interests of participants.[1]

The Japan-U.S. Businessmen's Conference has been meeting regularly since 1961 (see Table 8) yet has been less than successful in achieving a sufficiently cordial atmosphere to yield concrete results.[2] There are several reasons for this failure. First, the conference numbers up to 120 businessmen, too large for a meaningful give and take. Second, and opposite to the first, although the conference

TABLE 8

International Businessmen's Conferences, 1956-68

Region & Country	Total	56	57	58	59	60	61	62	63	64	65	66	67	68
Pacific Basin	19						2	2	1	2	4	2	4	2
United States	(15)						(2)	(1)		(2)	(3)	(2)	(3)	(2)
Canada	(4)							(1)	(1)		(1)		(1)	
Australia	(4)									(1)	(1)	(1)		(1)
Western Europe-USA	12								1	1	3	4	2	1
Western Europe	5										1		2	2
United Kingdon	(2)										(1)		(1)	
Germany (Fed. Repub.)	(2)												(1)	(1)
Sweden	(1)													(1)
East Asia	5											1	2	2
Korea (ROK)	(5)											(1)	(2)	(2)
Central America	2							1			1			
Mexico	(2)							(1)			(1)			
South Asia	1													1
India	(1)													(1)
Total	44						2	3	2	3	8	8	10	8

Note: Conferences involving one or two countries only are listed in parentheses and are also included in regional figures. The Western Europe-USA category consists of joint policy research conferences by: Doyukai; CED; CEPES of France, West Germany, Italy; PEP; SNS; SIE (see List of Abbreviations). Doyukai also participated in joint conferences with the United States (CED) and Australia (CEDA). Most of the other conferences are the responsibility of Keidanren.

Sources: Official reports of conferences; Ministry of Foreign Affairs, Waga gaiko no kinkyo [Present state of our foreign relations] (Tokyo: Ministry of Finance, annual); Keizai Doyukai and Keidanren staff interviews and documents, particularly "Kaigi haken keizai shisetsudanra hokokusho tenji mokuroku" [Catalog of reports on overseas economic missions and the like] (Tokyo: Keizai Dantai Rengokai, 1971); Japanese and English language newspapers.

is too inclusive the Japanese side is more representative of key organizations and individuals than is the American side.[3] The Japanese side is coordinated by Keidanren which can claim to represent Japanese business, while the United States side is led by the U.S. Chamber of Commerce which cannot represent American business, nor can any single organization. American business is just too big geographically, administratively, and politically. Third, discussions of key issues take the form of presenting each side's official positions and these are already known to the other side.

The result is often a debate between two belligerents trying to overpower each other, occasionally using veiled threats such as, "The U.S. delegation cited the possibility that solutions would be applied in the political sphere if appropriate steps were not taken to relieve the economic pressures."[4] Consequently, instead of moving the Japan-U.S. Businessmen's Conference toward the more formal commitments of a joint economic committee, business leaders on both sides established parallel organizations, recognizing that the American business community is too big and diffuse to be dealt with at any single organizational or geographic point.[5]

The Japanese business leader at the forefront of this trend was Yoshizane Iwasa, just as Shigeo Nagano was prominent in the formation of joint economic committees. In conjunction with Iwasa's economic mission to the United States in 1964, he and former Consul-General Wada in San Francisco saw that America's size and particularly its regional specialization and business community organization demanded a regional approach by Japan. They believed the first regional conference should not be with the New York-Boston business complex but on the West Coast where American businessmen had long been eager for closer economic ties with Japan. Furthermore, emphasis was to be on individual businessmen rather than on the organizations they represent, just as it is in Doyukai where Iwasa first became prominent. Favorable reaction from West Coast businessmen led to the formation of the Japan-California Association in 1964.

Following the same pattern of an economic mission preparing the ground for the formation of a regional conference, Kazutaka Kikawada's economic mission to the Midwest in June 1966 led to the formation of the Japan-Midwest Economic Conference in 1967.[6] He too is a Doyukai man and heads that organization. His response centering around the Chicago area was favorable, partly because Japan is such a good customer of Midwestern wheat and other agricultural products, and partly because the Midwest, being so far from either coast, had not had as many opportunities for international contact.

Lastly, a major Japanese mission to the American South was led by Masao Anzai of Showa Denko.[7] Out of it grew the Japan-South

Association. But despite these new regional approaches Japanese conference members still like to visit Washington as part of the itinerary. Like other participants in Japan's private economic diplomacy, they personally wish to meet foreign government officials.[8] The major contribution of international businessmen's conferences, however, lies in businessman-to-businessman rapport.

THE JAPAN-CALIFORNIA ASSOCIATION (JCA)

First launched in Ito, Japan, in October 1965, the Japan-California Association has since held regular annual meetings, alternating between Japan and California. Since JCA was created largely as the personal initiative of Iwasa, control of JCA remains in individual hands, as does its secretariat. Iwasa remains the co-chairman on the Japanese side, and to avoid bureaucratization, he chose to keep the Japanese secretariat at Fuji Bank rather than at one of the business associations.[9] On the American side, the co-chairmanship began with Rudolph Peterson, president of Bank of America, who passed it on in 1967 to Roy Ash, then president of Litton Industries. Administrative control of the American side, however, is held by Dr. Weldon Gibson, Executive Vice-President of Stanford Research Institute, where the secretariat for both JCA and PBEC is located. Financial control is similarly exercised, with member companies paying an annual fee through their respective JCA secretariats. Fees cover only meeting and secretariat expenses. Membership is open to company vice-presidents and up but must go through either Fuji Bank or SRI which gives these organizations their individually based, West Coast orientation.

In 1967, JCA members decided to expand its scope to Oregon, Washington, and British Columbia, although they did not change JCA's name.[10] Next JCA took personal contact a step further than most such business groups by adding a two-day conference for professional people at the level just below that of top executives. This innovation allowed more specialized discussions at the working level, but perhaps more important, established personal relationships among men who will be making key policy decisions later on.

A typical JCA meeting includes no more than twenty-five delegates from each side. Opening remarks by the two delegation leaders try to sort out the major issues and trends in U.S.-Japanese relations for the next year or so, more like keynote speeches than welcoming speeches. Then one speaker from each side, usually a banker, offers an analysis of the current status and outlook for his country's economy, with particular attention to growth rates, inflation, currency reserves, and balance of payments trends. Then the group breaks up into two or more discussion groups, with a rapporteur chosen to summarize the discussion when the groups rejoin. The topics vary only slightly from a general pattern: Protectionist legislation and practices in the United States, trade and capital liberalization measures in Japan, economic cooperation by industrialized nations with private enterprise in Southeast Asia, political and security issues between Japan and the United States, and problems of trade with the People's Republic of China.[11]

In the course of these discussions there will be much factual information exchanged; for example, the Japanese rule of thumb that a joint venture will take four to five years before showing a profit. But much of the discussion is policy oriented and stated as personal opinion so that it is possible to formulate, for purposes of company business or otherwise, a fairly good estimation of the men across the table. Summarizations at the end of the two day meetings pick out the main areas of agreement and disagreement without trying to reach a consensus.

Despite the unofficial nature of the discussions, the communicative process reaches official government circles both before and after conferences. In one example, bilateral negotiations over the textile issue had reached a stalemate and had been broken off. In the course of the JCA meeting in Kyoto of May 1970, the American members became aware of the desire of the Japanese government and business community to resume negotiations, and this observation was passed on to the White House. A short time later during a World Bank meeting in Copenhagen, the American Secretary of the Treasury received a call from the Japanese Finance Minister officially confirming Japan's desire to resume negotiations; meetings then reconvened almost immediately in Washington.[12] This was an example of the indirect way in which business can assist governmental communication through private economic diplomacy.

At the San Francisco meeting of JCA, co-chairman Ash of Litton Industries described the Nixon Administration as pragmatic in adopting measures toward free trade which it regards as a fundamentally desirable policy. He offered to serve as a channel of communication when he said, "The suggestions we make to our government in that vein (quid-pro-quo steps toward free trade) will get the greatest reception. We hope to take some from this meeting."[13]

In the same speech Ash quoted from a working paper by Dr. Gibson: "What is needed in our view is a series of steps designed to improve the overall 'economic climate' within which our respective companies can operate more effectively with each other."[14] Ash then broadened the idea from company to country: "It is our hope that, with such understanding we can each work in our countries to improve the climate for even more effective business and national

relations than we now have."[15] It is in this improvement of climate
that international businessmen's conferences can play a significant
role but which, by the same token, can be seriously counterproductive,
depending on how conferences are interpreted.

SIGNIFICANCE OF INTERNATIONAL
BUSINESSMEN'S CONFERENCES

Iwasa and his colleagues are not synonomous with Japan. He
is an internationalist business leader, which is only a part of the
zaikai, which is only a part of the business community, which is only
a part of Japan. JCA is one of the most careful associations to under-
line its own unofficial status, but there is always the danger that remarks repeated often enough at the conference table and in the press
become accepted as the majority view. This is not necessarily the
case.

When the lines are drawn clearly on an issue such as textiles,
it is relatively easy to identify the various interests involved and
their respective positions. But when general problems of tariffs and
nontariff barriers are discussed within a congenial atmosphere, an
American businessman is liable to come away feeling that the Japanese
have at last seen the light and will accelerate their liberalization
program. Then nothing happens, and what was a favorable economic
climate turns to disillusionment.

The cause is to be found in the composition of the economic
power structure and of the conference itself. Just as the Japanese
were disappointed to find that the U.S.-Japan Businessmen's Conference did not and could not represent the single touch point for the
levers of power in American business, the JCA or similar groups
tend to represent a special segment of the Japanese business community—the internationalist business leaders. Depending on the issue,
this may amount to half or less of all Japanese business leaders.

The mistake is comparable to accepting as actual practice or
promise what Doyukai says domestically when it speaks of social
responsibility for business. Then when nothing happens, writers
become disillusioned.[16] The fault is the writer's to think that Doyukai
speaks for business in the first place. It speaks to business, as does
JCA, and as do other conferences, joint committees, roving ambassadors, and economic missions. To achieve a favorable climate and
mutual understanding within these select groups is not necessarily
to achieve it in circles outside of internationalist business leaders.
Those who do attend conferences choose to do so because they already
possess a broad international persuasion.

In Chapter 2 we characterized seven internationalist business leaders and noted that none of them were identified with former zaibatsu groups, that their active participation in private economic diplomacy was not necessarily proportionate to their influence in business circles, in fact part of its purpose was to increase that influence. Yet the evidence did not support the corollary hypothesis that zaibatsu executives did not participate. On the lists of JCA participants you find such names as Norishige Hasegawa, president of Sumitomo Chemical; Tatsuzo Mizukami, president of Mitsui Trading; and Wataru Tajitsu, president of Mitsubishi Bank.[17] On other lists of the 176 events covered in this study, one finds the same names reappearing on other delegations, although seldom as delegation leaders because of the principle of equal distribution of honors among industrial groups. These names that reappear often, such as Hasegawa, become identified as internationalist business leaders, and their statements should be weighed accordingly.

One of the zaibatsu executives interviewed who generally chose not to participate was critical of the value of private economic diplomacy, charging in particular that government sponsored missions were "ceremonial." When pressed to elaborate on his reason for not participating he asked not to be identified and replied, "We are too busy," suggesting a bit facetiously that executives of firms such as Kikawada's Tokyo Electric Power might have more time available than executives of heavy industry. He also criticized Masao Anzai's mission to the U.S. South as "useless," but he singled out JCA as one of the more productive efforts in private economic diplomacy. He explained that JCA topics are selected and prepared in advance by Iwasa and Dr. Gibson so that actual talks are fruitful. Also there is a natural common interest between Japanese and West Coast businessmen. His judgment appeared to be based on where his company interests were located and whether they would benefit from business discussions in that particular area. On the other hand, the only man with more seniority in his company turned out to be quiet but active in JCA, PBEC, and several economic missions.* The choice is a personal one, based on an individual's perception of potential advantages to

---

*Although each business conference or joint committee has its own separate membership, many businessmen are members of several organizations, for example, JCA, PBEC, or the Japan-Australia Committee. A practice has developed to schedule some of these meetings consecutively, though not necessarily at the same location, enabling individuals to attend two meetings on one trip. In 1970, the above three groups scheduled meetings to coincide with a visit to Expo 70 at Kyoto.

the interests of his company and himself. In terms of personal prestige, the zaibatsu business leader has relatively less to gain because he already enjoys the prestige of his zaibatsu company name, a factor commonly accepted but impossible to measure.

Conferences can be attractive to individual interests because they allow for a higher degree of individual initiative. We have illustrated this primarily through the activities of Iwasa, although it also applies to other aspiring business leaders and to other forms of private economic diplomacy. Iwasa's success in becoming perhaps the leading Japanese businessman associated with Japan-U.S. economic affairs was achieved despite certain domestic shortcomings in his company base which precluded, say, becoming president of Keidanren. He did become one of seven Keidanren vice-presidents, but first he had to make his mark as a leader among the younger group of managers who founded Doyukai.

Upon approaching the top of their company ladder, men like Iwasa can add to their activity base through private economic diplomacy, and circumvent certain obstacles to the top of the traditional zaikai ladder by creating a new ladder—an internationalist one. It is this individual incentive which combines with other interests to produce Japan's private economic diplomacy.

NOTES

1. This is not to say that an international businessmen's conference cannot have diplomatic impact. A joint conference communique of the Japan-Mexico Economic Council in 1966 called on both governments to conclude a treaty of commerce and navigation and precipitated the negotiations which accomplished it in 1968. Japan Economic Journal, September 24, 1968, and Keidanren Review, No. 5 (1966), pp. 65-71.

2. Kiichiro Sato et al., "Minkan keizai gaiko no yakuwari to seika" [The role and results of private economic diplomacy], Keidanren Geppo, December 1967, p. 11. See also "Unfruitful Japan-U.S. Economic Confab," Oriental Economist, October 1971, p. 2.

3. The 1967 Japanese delegation was led for Keidanren by Ishizaka, and by Uemura, Nagano, Iwasa, and Kiichiro Sato, chairman of Mitsui Bank. The U.S. delegation was led by Allan Shivers, president of the U.S. Chamber of Commerce, and included George Champion, chairman of Chase Manhattan Bank, Fayette S. Dunn, president of Otis Elevator, and David M. Kennedy, chairman of Continental Banking. Japan Times, November 12, 1967.

4. Keidanren Review, No. 19 (1971), p. 9.

5. Doyukai, for example, has developed a fruitful joint policy study group relationship with the Committee for Economic Development (CED). These joint projects have generated several conferences which have been included in our statistical sample and which have produced significant policy studies. See Research and Policy Committee, East-West Trade: A Common Policy for the West (New York: Committee for Economic Development in association with Keizai Doyukai, CEPES—the European Committee for Economic and Social Progress, 1965), and Japan in the Free World Economy (With a Statement by Keizai Doyukai) (New York: Committee for Economic Development, 1963).

6. Japan Times, November 2, 1967. Kazutaka Kikawada and Thomas G. Ayers (president of the Chicago Chamber of Commerce and Industry) headed their respective delegations. Purposes and agenda paralleled that of the Japan-California Association except that more attention was given to agricultural trade and labor problems.

7. "Beikoku nambu homon keizai shisetsudan hokokusho [Report of the economic mission to the southern United States] (Tokyo: Beikoku nambu homon keizai shisetsudan, September 1969).

8. Based on interviews with Keidanren staff members and itineraries found in the reports listed in the bibliography.

9. Interview with Masahisa Segawa, Secretary to the President, the Fuji Bank Ltd., October 26, 1968.

10. "The Japan-California Association Report," SRI International, No. 13 (1969), p. 1.

11. "Japan-California Association Joint Statement," adopted at the third meeting, October 5-7, 1967, at Shima, Mie Prefecture, Japan. See also Asahi Evening News, October 7, 1967, p. 6. A brief history of JCA, issues on the agenda, and a list of participants are included.

12. Interview with Dr. Weldon B. Gibson, Executive Vice-President, Stanford Research Institute, and President, SRI International, November 6, 1971.

13. Opening remarks by Roy L. Ash, U.S. Co-Chairman of the Japan-California Association, in a special meeting in San Francisco, May 13, 1969.

14. Weldon B. Gibson, "The Japan-U.S. Partnership," Stanford Research Institute, May 13, 1969, p. 6.

15. Roy L. Ash, opening remarks.

16. See, for example, Yuichiro Noguchi, "Yotsu no keieisha dantai" [Four business associations] (Chuo Koron, October 1960), pp. 164-65. According to Noguchi, "It is no exaggeration to say that Keizai Doyukai leads the financial world." In this study we have assumed no single point of leadership, rather a cluster of cooperative-competitive groups and individuals.

17. "Record of the First Meeting of the Japan-California Association" (Menlo Park: Stanford Research Institute, November 1965).

7

An overall evaluation of private economic diplomacy can only be approximated since the primary objective is a favorable economic climate, a goal which is both hard to maintain and hard to measure. We have found scattered instances during 1956-68 of reparations agreements signed, trade barriers reduced, investment understanding reached, contracts negotiated, and policy information gathered. However, the Japanese place the establishment of a favorable climate first, after which tangible steps can be taken.[1]

The causal factor in Japan's improved bilateral and multilateral relations is not immediately apparent because of the time element. Private economic diplomacy, like traditional diplomacy, requires much time and repetition to bear fruit. In this respect it performs a seeding role for professional diplomacy which matures much later, sometimes years later. When Shigeo Nagano led a mission to the USSR in 1958 he raised the possibility of a Tokyo-Moscow air route. Gradually this was achieved through constant efforts of the Foreign Ministry, including economic missions, and the Transportation Ministry. Not until March 1970 did Japan Air Lines pilots begin to fly without Russian supervision over Siberia—up to that time an area too sensitive for the Russians.[2] As another example, the Japanese idea of regional discussions within the United States began brewing sometime in 1963, was proposed during the Iwasa Mission in 1964, but took five years to evolve from JCA to the Japan-South Association, the third such regional association. Private economic diplomacy takes time, but it does provide the channels of communication to bring about tangible results. We shall briefly examine some statistical indications of tangible economic progress without attempting to demonstrate a direct cause and effect relationship.

If we look at the growth rate of gross national product during the thirteen-year period of our study, 1956-68, we find that GNP grew at a real annual rate of 10.2 percent and Japan became the world's third ranking industrial power.[3] As a trading nation, Japan moved in world rank from ninth in 1959 to fifth in 1968, ahead of France but behind the United States, West Germany, the United Kingdom, and Canada.[4]

We can also compare Japan's bilateral trade with her economic goals, one of which was to decrease dependence on the United States or any single nation by increasing economic relations with as many countries as possible while maintaining, even increasing, her American market. Japanese writers and business leaders interviewed agreed on the importance of this goal. The regional distribution of events in Appendix B shows considerable priority for industrialized Pacific Basin countries (fifty-eight events) and for Western Europe (forty-four), with the United States (thirty-eight) still retaining highest country priority and the Soviet Union (eight) on the low side. This set of priorities for private economic diplomacy correlates fairly well with actual trade figures. As of 1968, 37.9 percent of Japan's exports went to Pacific Basin countries of which 31 percent went to the United States. Japan's exports to Europe remained small in 1968, only 12.7 percent of total exports, but by 1970 this was up to 15 percent.[5]

The effort toward joint development of Siberia had little effect, if any, by 1968. Although Japan passed Finland and Britain in 1968 to become the Soviet Union's leading Free World supplier, Japan-Soviet trade was still only one-twelfth of Japan-U.S. trade.[6] So progress toward less dependence, given the natural inclination to continue expanding the U.S. market, is most evident in qualitative terms such as access to critical raw materials. Before 1956 Japan had imported 83 percent of her foreign coal from the United States. By 1968 these imports had been cut in half and the Japan Iron and Steel Federation estimated that half of Japan's imported coal would soon be coming from Australia.[7] These data indicate that Japan's priorities for private economic diplomacy as tabulated in Appendix B roughly approximate her diplomatic goals as perceived by businessmen and trends in Japanese trade figures for 1968.

If we measure results in terms of public image—the economic animal syndrome—then clearly Japanese private economic diplomacy has failed. Despite numerous missions, roving ambassadors, and the like, the Japanese businessman in 1968 was respected but not well liked, and his image has further deteriorated since.[8] Japanese businessmen worked hard and were respected both for personal conduct and for high quality goods, but their motivation was still thought to be strictly commercial. Perhaps there were growing conflicts of interest between Japan and other countries which defied diplomatic solutions.[9] More likely, there may be limitations built into Japan's system which has proved so successful in terms of economic growth.

There are two factors working against Japan, one cultural and the other structural. Culturally, the homogeneity that allows the Japanese to work together so well also sets them apart in what Lawrence Olson calls Japan's "human isolation from the rest of the world." They do not assimilate well, for example, in Singapore where they have their own clubs and schools.[10] Private economic diplomacy has not alleviated this problem except at the elite level where business leaders do develop close friendships with foreigners but always from a comfortable base at home.

Structurally, the progress made at the diplomatic level apparently fails to sift down to the trader in the field. Thus the advantages gained by the elite system are offset by the lack of exposure of more junior executives to noncommercial aspects of international trade. The man in the field is given only the responsibility to sell. This he does well at the cost, sometimes, of cordial relations with the people of the host country.

To alleviate the situation, the Japan External Trade Organization (JETRO) urged Japanese companies to pay more attention to public relations activities.[11] Such measures most likely will not solve the problem until the distinction between business leader and trader, between the economic and the commercial, is reduced through broader responsibility and management training at the lower levels.

The economic/commercial distinction fits naturally into the Japanese management pattern of hard competition as juniors followed by released time at the president level and above. The practice of utilizing business leaders as diplomats also helps perpetuate those relatively few individuals at the top. In so doing it may widen the gap (for example, communication, credibility) between what business-men-diplomats say and do, and what businessmen-salesmen say and do. This is why the "economic animal" problem persists, that is, Japanese elites reach only other elites, not the general public in Japan or in other countries. There is much more work still to be done, particularly in exposing more middle level managers (as JCA does) to the give and take of international discussions on broad policy problems not directly related to company sales. However, as long as economic and commercial activities are conducted by different individuals and events, there will be a finite limit on achieving objectives such as improving Japan's image, even while the same system facilitates communication and policy-making among elites.

LIMITATIONS OF INTERNATIONALIST BUSINESS LEADERS

Business leaders like Iwasa and Nagano may indeed think more of the national interest and even of world peace than they do of company or personal profit. Nevertheless, it is not unkind to say that they can afford to do so, having advanced to positions of wealth and power through their respective social, company, and activity bases. While our empirical data showed considerable growth for private economic diplomacy, the key participants remain only a handful of internationally oriented men.

Although these men are active in private economic diplomacy they are not the only powers within the business community.[12] They are sort of super ambassadors for the business community, and as such, increase their status up to a point but other factors such as the type of company power base ultimately govern their upper limits of power. These modern captains-of-industry are hired managers, not owners of their corporations. They must compete with their peers through managerial ability plus the traditional channels of school and marriage ties, political skill with Diet members and bureaucrats, and sheer hard work. The men who enter management after the war and made it to the top, notably Masaru Ibuka of Sony among others, have not yet replaced traditional leadership circles. Ask a Japanese to name the top electronic firms and he will mention Hitachi and Toshiba, perhaps Matsushita, but never Sony. A foreigner might well reply in reverse order. Behind-the-scenes power may pass to less traditional quarters, but only very slowly. This is why a Japanese can honestly say that Yoshizane Iwasa, one of the world's more influential men in international banking, was weaker domestically in terms of power at the top of the Japanese business community. At the age of 62 in 1968 Iwasa was a newcomer compared to the elders (choro) of the business community who retained top prestige if not top political influence.

Even if not as influential as one might assume from the English language press, the internationalist business leader does have the international contacts and institutional channels to deal with crisis situations such as a sudden worsening of the balance of payments problem. He has a global frame of reference and can understand how foreigners think. Working through private economic diplomacy he can at least keep the dialogue open, and keep the economic climate as favorable as conditions will allow.

In the long term, however, the internationalist business leader may not be able to effect the domestic changes that are required for any real solution. He no longer runs his company on a day to day basis, for the system delegates much authority to those just under the president level. On the other hand, it is unlikely that he controls majority opinion among his peers, even if he is an officer of a major business association. It is vital that foreign businessmen and government officials understand this pluralism, otherwise the many meetings and wide press afforded internationalist business leaders will invite

100

false expectations among foreigners, and subsequent disillusionment. The realization of change will continue to depend on serving a wide range of interests among groups and individuals.

A CLUSTER OF UNDERLYING INTERESTS

Among government ministries, the responsibility and interests of the Foreign Ministry were paramount, followed by MITI, and other ministries and agencies as appropriate. We found that the Foreign Ministry benefited, in addition to whatever was achieved in the host country, by utilizing business leader participants as sources of information and support vis-a-vis other ministries and policy bodies. This will work only so long as participation is also to the advantage of the individual.

In the individual's interest, private economic diplomacy serves as both a recognition of status and as an activity base for advancing one's personal views and career. Business leaders who participate are often the same individuals who are influential in advisory groups, study groups, faction support groups, and business associations. While it cannot be documented here, it is easy to imagine a sequence of communication like this: A business leader develops some information or a policy position while on an economic mission. He sees that that position is included in the mission report which is then circulated to governmental agencies and business associations. He follows up by supporting his position at meetings of advisory groups such as the Economic Deliberation Council, study groups such as the Industrial Problems Research Society, factional support groups such as Choeikai,[13] and committees of business associations such as Keidanren. The extent to which his position is accepted depends not only on the merit of his position but on the scope of his influence— social base, company base, and activity base. He will use these as leverage to muster a consensus for his position among business and government circles. His position may remain only a position or be accepted—however modified—as official policy, whereupon it returns as such to the diplomatic level, including subsequent events of private economic diplomacy. As a result, the individual business leader gains in policy influence and prestige, and the participating ministry broadens its base of support.

The growth of private economic diplomacy to 1968 attests to the fact that participant interests continued to be served, and to that extent the overall interest as well. It does not necessarily follow that the cluster of mutual interests between ministries, business associations, and individuals which marked 1956-68 will continue into the 1970s and beyond. The degree of cooperation depends not only on a shared overall interest but a need for each other. The mutual need for our period of study was a carryover from defeat in the war, the Occupation (under which Japan was not allowed its own diplomacy), and the need for exports to strengthen the economy. The military had been removed as a power bloc, and neither the Diet, the bureaucracy, nor business could achieve their goals on their own strength.

A subjective reading of the interviews and literature for this study to 1968 confirmed a latent insecurity among Japanese businessmen about the outlook for private enterprise—the keystone of Japanese business ideology.[14] That is one reason Ishizaka and others preferred to deal with countries where private enterprise was strong, and only secondarily with neighboring Communist China and the USSR. When leftist parties called for a reorientation away from dependence on the United States, toward normalization with Communist countries, business leaders strove to improve American-Japanese understanding to the point where economic and political fluctuations would not upset long term close relations. They knew that recessions and world monetary crises, the Okinawa and Mutual Security Treaty issues, and the resurgence of protectionism centering on textiles could put the relationship into serious disarray. It is this that the Japanese business community was working to avoid.

In the late 1960s, however, businessmen themselves began to have doubts about dependence on a single country. And since 1968, the whole rationale of high growth in GNP and exports has been undermined by inflation, pollution, and social problems which will test cooperation between government and business.

In response to their own desire to strengthen private enterprise, and to diversify their trade and investment, Japanese businessmen began to build their own institutions which would enable them, among other things, to conduct their own private economic diplomacy. Such a trend is discernible in the overall pattern of events (see Table 9) by comparing the growth of the first two types, which government sponsors, to the latter two types, which it does not.

The Economic Mission

The economic mission has been the most widely used approach, although its use reached a peak in 1962 and dropped off sharply in 1967 when the business world began to act more on its own initiative through joint committees and conferences in addition to government sponsored missions.* The economic mission form is used to improve

---

*The drop-off might be due in part to reaching the saturation point in certain countries. An American foreign service officer and

102

TABLE 9

Private Economic Diplomacy by Type, 1956-68

Type	Total	1956	1957	1958	1959	1960	1961	1962	1963	1964	1965	1966	1967	1968
Economic missions	85	4		3	2	8	10	12	7	9	9	10	4	7
Roving Ambassador appointments	9	1	4	3									1	
Joint economic committee meetings	39		2	1		2	1	3	2	3	3	5	8	9
International businessmen's conferences	43						2	3	2	3	8	8	10	7
Total	176	5	6	7	2	10	13	18	11	15	20	23	23	23

Sources: Official reports; Ministry of Foreign Affairs, Waga gaiko no kinkyo [Present state of our foreign relations] (Tokyo: Ministry of Finance, annual); Keizai Doyukai and Keidanren staff interviews and documents, particularly "Kaigi haken keizai shisetsudanra hokokusho tenji mokuroku" [Catalog of reports on overseas economic missions and the like] (Tokyo: Keizai Dantai Rengokai, 1971); Japanese and English language newspapers.

103

Japan's image, remove obstacles to trade and investment, and gather information. Its small number of delegates provides optimum capability to work as a team on specific bilateral problems or to establish better relations with developing countries with which Japan does not yet have the degree of economic interchange necessary to support regular joint committees and conferences. Once missions and other forms of interchange have built up economic relations in a given country, economic missions can be reserved for trouble-shooting, as in the 1968 Kiichiro Sato mission to the United States to head off the import surcharge.[15]

The Roving Ambassador

The roving ambassador approach was of limited value because a single lay diplomat trying to cover an entire region in a one-shot tour lacks depth. But it is there for use if and when the situation calls for it. The trend of late has been to use party politicians rather than businessmen in this capacity. There is no inclination to use regular or retired diplomats as roving ambassador trouble-shooters as the United States has sometimes done.

The use of businessmen as roving ambassadors made its contribution of developing a regional approach to several countries by means of a short period of intensive travel. It proved useful in negotiating agreements, improving Japan's image, and gathering information. It will most likely be used hereafter only in spot situations or for groupings of smaller countries.

The Joint Economic Committee

The joint economic committee is generally used where active relations have already been established with a given country and both sides desire to institutionalize the relationship, at least to the extent of providing a forum for regularly held discussions.* Once established,

---

a Japanese company vice-president remarked in separate interviews that there were too many missions to the United States (by which they meant those that include Washington, D.C.,) in the itinerary in order to meet the highest ranking officials possible.

*As a sponsoring institution and forum locale, Keidanren remains the principal Japanese organization behind the joint committee structure. Keidanren itself is a giant pyramid of committees, and its Tokyo headquarters building includes lavish conference, dining, and library facilities.

a relatively inactive joint committee like the Japan-Argentina committee may not meet every year but it stays on the books. In this manner the number of joint committee meetings rises to a plateau, then rises again, as new committees are created. Joint committee meetings will increase in absolute terms, but not necessarily in relation to other approaches, for needs will continue to vary for the business community, the Foreign Ministry, and the countries and individuals involved. The need for a joint committee to negotiate agreements as in the Japan-Soviet committee is rare but, except for the limitations of formality, the joint committee form offers year-to-year continuity and depth.

The International Businessmen's Conference

The international businessmen's conference has grown in popularity because of its flexibility and informality. While the number of conferences was minimal to 1964, it then rose sharply, thanks largely to Doyukai's joint policy conferences with similar organizations in the United States and Europe. With the increasing need for multilateral aid and investment in developing countries, multilateral businessmen's conferences grew proportionately because there were few existing structure for such action in the private sector. Also, the conference is the most flexible of the four types of private economic diplomacy because it can be one-shot or periodic, small group or larger group requiring several hotels.* It is likely, therefore, to continue its steady rise in usage, just as is happening throughout the diplomatic community. It should be considered a middle level approach between the economic mission which establishes the basis for good trade relations, and the joint economic committee which institutionalizes and expands those established relations under business sponsorship.

The gradual evolution of this trend will both strengthen the business community (short of uniting it) relative to other domestic foreign policy elites, and create stronger cross-national business ties, an international fraternity of business elites, similar to that now functioning in many scientific disciplines. These cross-national personal and institutional business ties can resolve or exacerbate problems between governments, depending on a constructive but realistic utilization of the internationalist business leader.

---

*The Japanese delegation is usually quite large when an international businessmen's conference is held in Japan, but the first working level conference of JCA had only 35 delegates, divided 18 and 17 Japanese and American, respectively. Not surprisingly, the smaller size conference appears to be the most effective.

Fundamental changes required in the international trade and monetary system are already in progress, with private economic diplomacy playing a discussant role. But some of the most fundamental changes must take place within Japan itself, such as the acceptance of foreign management in Japanese companies. One of our main findings was the role played by private economic diplomacy as an instrument to bring about domestic change, an instrument used by internationally minded groups and individuals within Japanese business and government to influence their own national policy as in the Takasugi and Kobayashi Reports.

Internationally, now that Japan is faced with the need to assume the political and social responsibilities of a world economic power, the Japanese businessman as a diplomatic animal (viz an economic animal) has his task cut out for him: to broaden his image and his actual performace. Our study has analyzed one way he does this—by private economic diplomacy.

NOTES

1. "Active Private Economic Diplomacy Developing," Asahi Evening News, special supplement, May 13, 1969, p. 2. This supplement was published on the occasion of the Second General Meeting of PBEC and contains a review of Japan's meetings with American businessmen and statements by business leaders such as the following quotation from Kazutaka Kikawada's April 17 address to the annual meeting of Doyukai: "Japan finds herself in a position to play an important role in promoting international cooperation. The time has come for us to push ahead with systematic expansion of private economic diplomacy."

2. Japan Times, September 27, 1968, p. 12; October 23, p. 11; October 30, p. 8. The Nagano roving ambassadorship of 1958 was described as "spade work" for the Tokyo-Moscow air route agreement of 1969. Interview with Yasuo Takeyama, Chief, Editorial Staff, Nihon Keizai Shimbun, February 18, 1969.

3. Kuranosuke Saito, "Characteristic Features of Japan's Economic Development," Fuji Bank Bulletin, December 1969, p. 209.

4. Japan Times, February 28, 1969, p. 8.

5. Economic Affairs Bureau, Ministry of Foreign Affairs, Statistical Survey of Japan's Economy, 1971 (Tokyo: Ministry of Foreign Affairs), p. 43.

6. Oriental Economist, Vol. 37, No. 700 (February 1969), p. 49.

7. Japan Times, December 16, 1968, p. 9.

8. Examples of Japan's bad press are numerous: "How to Cope with Japan's Business Invasion," Time, May 10, 1971; "Europe: Facing

the 'Yellow Peril'," Far Eastern Economic Review, February 27, 1971; "Japan-U.S. Mentality Gap," San Francisco Chronicle, June 6, 1969, p. 9E; and "Japan's Firm Diplomacy Towards Southeast Asia Urged," Mainichi, April 16, 1971, p. 2.

9. For a country-by-country discussion of Japanese short-comings to 1968 see Chapter V of Lawrence Olson, Japan in Postwar Asia (New York: Praeger, 1970).

10. Olson, Ibid., pp. 201, 202, 210.

11. Far Eastern Economic Review, March 13, 1971, p. 74.

12. This paragraph is based on interviews with Kiichi Miyazawa, Member of the Diet and Director General, Economic Planning Agency, March 10, 1969, and with Kunio Okabe, Foreign Affairs Department, Yawata Iron and Steel Co., March 1 and 5, 1969.

13. Nathaniel Thayer, How the Conservatives Rule Japan (Princeton: Princeton University Press, 1969), pp. 65-66. The Choeikai which supported Premier Sato was one of many such factional support groups. They meet regularly, usually monthly, for informal discussions on current policy issues.

14. Our attention was first called to this attitude within the Japanese business community in an interview with Masahisa Segawa, Secretary to the President, The Fuji Bank, Ltd., October 26, 1968. See also "Seijishoku ga takamaru zaikai minkan gaiko" [Political coloring deepens in private economic diplomacy], Keizai Tembo, October 1, 1968, p. 19.

15. 'Ho Bei keizai shisetsudan kaku kaidan kiroku" [Complete conference record of the economic mission to the United States] (Tokyo: Secretariat of the Economic Mission to the United States, April 1968).

APPENDIX A

Private Economic Diplomacy by Date, 1956-68

(economic missions, roving ambassadors, joint economic committee meetings, and
international businessmen's conferences)

Date	Purpose	Chairman	Type	Remarks
		1956		
3/21 (1 mo.)	Econo. coop. w/SE	Uemura Kogoro VP, Keidanren	P	South Vietnam, Cambodia, Thailand, Burma, Pakistan
4/17	Reparations	Fujiyama Aiichiro Pr., Nissho	A	Philippines
6/18	Small business	Ayukawa Yoshiike Pr., Med. Small Inds.	G	Indonesia
7/3-8/18	2d trade mission to China	Ito Kesaichi, Intl. Trade Prom. Assoc.	P	Communist China
8/13	Reparations	Fujiyama Aiichiro Pr., Nissho	G	Philippines
		1957		
4	1st, Cmte for Prom of Taiwan-J Coop.	Fujiyama Aiichiro Pr., Nissho	J	Cmte. estab. 4/57
8/10-10/12	L. Amer. rels.	Shibusawa Keizo Ch., Intl Tel & Tel	A	Mexico, Uruguay, Argentina, Paraguay, Chile, Bolivia, Panama, Colombia, Venezuela, Dominican Republic, Cuba
9/10-10/26	Near & Mid. East	Ito Takeo Pr., OSK Line	A	Egypt, Syria, Iraq, Ethiopia, Sudan, Saudi Arabia, Lebanon, Jordan, Turkey, Iran

Date	Leader	Purpose		Countries/Notes
9/20–11/16	Hotta Shozo, Pr., Sumitomo Bank	W. Eur. rels.	A	Denmark, Sweden, Germany, Switzerland, Austria, Yugoslavia, United Kingdom, Belgium, France, Spain, Italy, Greece, Israel
10	Adachi Tadashi, Pr., Nissho	Cmte for Prom. of Taiwan-J Coop.	J	Taipei, 2d meeting
11/24	Kobayashi Ataru, Pr., Overseas Tech Coop. Agency	SE Asia rels.	A	Thailand, Burma, Pakistan, India, Ceylon, Singapore, Indonesia, Vietnam, Cambodia, Philippines, Hong Kong

1958

Date	Leader	Purpose		Countries/Notes
1/1 (ret.)	Uemura Kogoro, VP, Keidanren	Reparations	A	unsuccessful
5 or 6	Adachi Tadashi, Pr., Nissho	Cmte for Prom. of Taiwan-J Coop.	J	Tokyo, 3rd meeting
9/5	Nagano Shigeo, Pr., Fuji Iron & Steel	NE Europe trade	A	USSR, Poland, Czechoslovakia, Denmark, Finland, Norway, Sweden
9 (3 wks)	Ito Chubei, Ch., Toyo Pulp	Machinery exports	G	Australia, New Zealand
9 (3 wks)	Sasabe Kureo, Pr., Nagoya Ch. of Commerce	Textiles, sundries	G	Denmark, Norway, Sweden, Netherlands, Belgium, West Germany, France, United Kingdom, Switzerland, Italy, Austria
10/7 (40 days)	Inagaki Heitaro, Pr., J for Trade Coun.	First trade mission to U.S. & Canada	G	12 U.S. cities & 4 Canadian
10/21	Tobata Seiichi	Mid. East & SE Asia rels.	A	13 countries

(continued)

Appendix A (continued)

Date	Purpose	Chairman	Type	Remarks
1	Cmte for Prom. of Taiwan-J Coop.	Adachi Tadashi Pr., Nissho	J	Taipei, 4th meeting
		1959		
10 (4 wks)	Heavy mach. exps. to Caribbean	Miura Fumio, Pr. L. Amer. Friendship Society	G	Mexico, Guatemala, El Salvador, Costa Rica, Panama, Ecuador, Colombia, Venezuela, Dominican Republic, Haiti, Cuba
10/15	Cmte for Prom. of Taiwan-J Coop.	Andachi Tadashi Pr., Nissho	J	Tokyo, 5th meeting
10/24 (34 days)	2nd Trade Mission to U.S.	Okamatsu Seitaro Pr., Chiyoda Manufac.	G	Emphasis on Midwest & South; 10 cities
		1960		
1/31	NA	Yamamoto ex-V Min. For. Affs.	P	
3/9- 4/2	Econ. coop. survey	Kagawa Hideshi Pr., Toyo Menka	G	Ghana, Nigeria
3/15 (2 mos)	Trade barriers in Mediterranean	Shoji Takeo, Pr. Asahi Electro. Chem.	G	Egypt, Sudan, Greece, Turkey, Yugoslavia, Italy, Tunisia, Morocco, Portugal, Spain
3/24- 4/6	Negotiate rice imports	Morinaga Teiichiro Pr., Med. Small Inds. Financial Bank	G	Burma
9 (2 wks)	Econo. coop. & trade	Muto Itoji, Pr., Kanebo	G	Iran

Date	Activity	Person	Type	Countries/Notes
9/12-10	1st Doyukai survey Eur. integration	Mizukami Tatsuzo Pr., Mitsui Trading	P	Belgium, France, Italy, Netherlands, West Germany, United Kingdom, & 4 other EFTA countries
10/8 (3 wks)	L–T trade	Takasaki Tatsunosuke	P	Communist China
10	Survey Mid. East primary products	Asami Seiichi Mitsuibishi Trading	G	* —

1961

Date	Activity	Person	Type	Countries/Notes
1/10-1/13	Cmte for Prom. of Taiwan–J Coop.	Adachi Tadashi Pr., Nissho	J	Tokyo, 6th meeting
2/23-3/11	Survey trade & industry prom.	Kai Fumihiko Dir., JETRO	G	Kenya, Uganda, Tanganyika
2/ (1 mo)	Survey for econo. coop.	Watanabe Takeshi, Pr., Asian Devel. Bank	P	India, Pakistan, Ceylon, Singapore, Malaysia, Thailand
2/26 (1 wk)	Econo. coop. & goodwill	Uemura Kogoro VP, Keidanren	P	Nationalist China, also Okinawa
2/28-3/16	"Deepen mutual understanding"	Nagano Shigeo, Pr., Fuji Iron & Steel	P	Australia, New Zealand, Nagano proposed J–Aust. Bus. Coop. Cmte.
3/30 (28 days)	3rd mission to U.S. & Canada: trade & labor problems	Sato Kiichiro Pr., Mitsui Bank	G	6 U.S. cities & Montreal, Ottawa
4 (2 wks)	Survey 2d 5 year plan	Niwa Kaneo, Pr., J–Pakistan Assoc.	G	Pakistan
9 (2 wks)	Private base for econ. coop.	Iwasa Yoshizane Pr., Fuji Bank	P	Canada
9/29-10/28	2d Doyukai survey of W. Eur. integration	Ninomiya Yoshimoto Pr., Toyo Soda Mfg.	P	Netherlands, Belgium, France, Italy, West Germany, United Kingdom

(continued)

Appendix A (continued)

Date	Purpose	Chairman	Type	Remarks
10/17	Joint policy res.	Iwasa Yoshizane Pr., Fuji Bank	C	United States (San Francisco)
11/7-11/9	J-U.S. Businessmen's Conf.	Ishizaka Taizo Pr., Keidanren	C	Tokyo, 1st meeting
NA	Primary products & tech. coop.	Ushiba, Bur. Chief Min. For. Affs.	G	Nigeria, Incl. businessmen
12/10-(50 days)	Arabian peninsula mkts., tech. coop.	Miyata Takaichiro	G	Kuwait, Saudi Arabia, Bahrein, Kataru, Oman, Aden, Yemen, Somalia
12	J-Mexico Econ. Council trade imbalance	Izawa Minoru, Gen. Mgr., L. Amer. Society	C	Mexico City, 1st meeting
		1962		
1	Cmte. for Prom. of Taiwan-J Coop.	Ishii Mitsujiro politician	J	Taipei, 7th meeting
2/20	Tax-free exports of raw mat. & facilities to ROK	Yukawa Kohei, Pr., Korean Industry Prom. Co.	P	ROK. Prelim. talks
3/3 (5 wks)	Anti-J trade discr. Cent. Amer. Cmn. Mkt.	Terao Ichiro, Man. Dir., Mitsubishi Trading	G	Mexico, Guatemala, El Salvador, Nicaragua, Panama, Dominican Republic, Haiti. Successful vs. Guat. trade discr; commerc. agreements w/El Sal., Mex.
6/21 (1 mo)	Inspect Soviet industries	Shimamoto Toru, Pr., Bank of Hokkaido	P	USSR
6/27-6/28	Joint policy res. Doyukai w/CED	Iwasa Yoshizane Pr., Fuji Bank	J	San Francisco: toward "J in the Free World Economy"

Date	Activity	Person		Notes
8/21 (1 mo)	Sign $96 million ship sales w/USSR; inspect Sov. ind.	Kawai Yoshinari Ch., Komatsu Mfg.	P	Kawai proposed to Khrushchev the joint devel. of Siberia
9/3	Econ. coop. survey	Takasugi Shinichi Advisor, Mitsubishi Electric	G	Malaysia. Reported govt. stable for aid.
9/15 (38 days)	4th mission to U.S. & Canada; trade	Suzuki Kyoichi Ch., Tokai Bank	G	11 U.S. & 4 Canadian cities
9/22-10/5	Survey Eur. econ. integration	Ichikawa Shinobu Pr., Marubeni Iida	P	For Osaka Ch. of Commerce
10	J-Canada Businessmen's Conf.	Horikoshi Teizo Dir-gen., Keidanren	C	Tokyo, Osaka; 1st meeting
10/11-10/26	Italian discrim. vs. J exports	Doi Masaharu, Pr., Sumitomo Chem.	G	Considered unsuccessful because of excessive formality
10/17-10/18	Joint policy res., Doyukai w/CED	Mizukami Tatsuzo Pr., Mitsui Trading	J	Tokyo, 2d meeting toward "in the Free World Economy"
10/18-11/9	High level talks in W. Eur.	Ishizaka Taizo Pr., Keidanren	G	Denmark, West Germany, France, Belgium, Netherlands
10/21-11/20	Reciprocate 4/62s mission from UK	Adachi Tadashi Pr., Nissho	P	London; Later institutionalized as a Conference
10/26	L-T trade	Takasaki Tatsunosuke	P	Communist China
11/19-11/21	J-U.S. Businessmen's Conf. bal. of payments, com. bloc trade	Sato Kiichiro	C	Washington, D.C., 2d meeting
12-1/63	Mkts. & discrim. in Fr. & Belgian Africa	Okajima Yoshiyuki Ch., Nichimen Cotton	G	Madagascar, Brazzaville, Leopoldville, Cameroons, Togo, Dahomey, Upper Volta, Nigeria, Ivory Coast, Liberia, Guinea, Senegal

(continued)

113

Appendix A (continued)

1963

Date	Purpose	Chairman	Type	Remarks
3/15-4/9	3d Doyukai survey of Eur. integration	Inoue Hidehiro Pr., Nihon Cement	P	France, Italy, West Germany, Netherlands, Belgium, United Kingdom, Greece, Switzerland, EEC, OECD, GATT, CEPES
5/16-6/2	J-Australia Joint Cmte.	Adachi Tadashi Pr., Nissho	J	Tokyo, 1st meeting
5	Cmte. for Prom. of J-Taiwan Coop.	Adachi Tadashi Pr., Nissho	J	Tokyo, 8th meeting
9/9-10/4	Trade promotion, survey LAFTA	Kawada Shige Pr., J. Steel Tube	G	Colombia, Peru, Ecuador, Bolivia, Chile
9/14 (2 wks)	NA	Okazaki Kaheita Pr., All J. Airways	P	Communist China
9/17-10/6	Talks with top management in Europe	Takeuchi Shunichi Pr., Mitsubishi Oil	P	Japan Productivity Center sponsored
9/25-10/1	Survey E-W trade	Wada Tsunesuke Pr., Fujitsu	G	Yugoslavia, Rumania, Bulgaria
10/13-10/22	J-Canada Businessmen's Conf.	Kawada Shige Pr., J. Steel Tube	C	Canada, 2d meeting
10/17-10/18	Doyukai w/CED, CEPES of Fr., Ger., Ital., PEP, SNS, SIE (Spain)	Kikawada Kazutaka Pr., Tokyo Elec. Power	C	Tokyo, on 'Growth of the World Economy'
10/18	Survey Eur. integr: monetary, securities, wages, labor, imports	Aoba Fumio Dir-gen, Fuji Bank	G	West Germany, France, Italy, Netherlands, Belgium, Luxembourg, United Kingdom, Switzerland

Date	Activity	Person		Details
10/20–11/16	Trade promotion w/EFTA	Hotta Shozo Pr., Sumitomo Bank	G	1st to EFTA: Denmark, Norway, Sweden, Finland, Austria, Switzerland, Spain, Portugal, United Kingdom

1964

Date	Activity	Person		Details
1	Econ. coop.	Nakayama Sohei Pr., Indust. Bank of J.	P	Pakistan, India, Taiwan, Malaysia, Thailand
2/20	Survey devel. for trade policy & legislation	Koizumi Yukihisa Ch., Furukawa Elec.	G	North Africa: Morocco, Algeria, Tunisia, Liberia, Saudi Arabia, Sudan, Turkey
3/20–4/18	Wider coverage of U.S.	Iwasa Yoshizane Pr., Fuji Bank	G	13 U.S. cities, led to J-Calif. Assoc.
4	J-Italy Joint Econ. Cmte.	Doi Masaharu Ch., Sumitomo Chem.	J	Tokyo, 1st meeting
5	J-U.S. Businessmen's Conf.	Adachi Tadashi Pr., Nissho	C	Tokyo, 3d meeting
6	W. Eur. econ. coop. w/devel. nations	Nakayama Sohei Pr., Indust. Bank of J.	P	2d J. Productivity Center Mission to Eur.
7	Doyukai joint res. on "East-West Trade"	NA	C	7 grps. of Western Europe, United States, Japan
9/2–9/3	J-Australia Joint Econ. Cmte.	Adachi Tadashi Pr., Nissho	J	Canberra, 2d meeting: Aust. proposed idea of PBECC.
9/14	Doyukai joint grp. on Phil., Thai. case studies, SE Asia devel.	Kikawada Kazutaka Pr., Tokyo Elec. Power	C	Tokyo, 1st study grp. meet. of Doyukai, CED, CEDA.
10/4–10/29	Wider coverage of Canada	Inayama Yoshihiro Pr., Yawata Steel	G	Vancouver, Victoria, Calgary, Edmonton, Regina, Winnipeg, Toronto, Ottawa, Montreal, Quebec

(continued)

Appendix A (continued)

Date	Purpose	Chairman	Type	Remarks
10/6 (3 wks)	SE Asian relations	Ichikawa Shinobu Ch., Marubeni Iida	G	Philippines, Malaysia, Thailand, Indonesia, Taiwan, Singapore
10/17-11	W. Eur. primary products & econ. integ.	Fukunaga Toshiyuki ed. staff, Nihon Keizai Shimbun	G	Belgium, West Germany, Italy, France, Luxembourg, United Kingdom, Netherlands, Switzerland, Austria, Sweden, Greece
10/29-11	Commercial rels. w/UK, Portugal, Spain	Yanagi Masuo Pr., Mitsui Bank	P	United Kingdom, Portugal, Spain; by Nissho & Tokyo Chamb. of Commerce
11/1-11/20	"E. Eur. in Transfiguration"; surv. coexistence & Sov.-Chinese rels.	Kosaka Tokusaburo Pr., Shin-etsu Chem.	G	Poland, Czechoslovakia, Hungary
12/6	Cmte. for Prom. of Taiwan-J Coop.	Sato Kiichiro Pr., Mitsui Bank	J	Taipei, 9th meeting
		1965		
NA	Cmte. for Prom. of Taiwan-J. Coop.	Adachi Tadashi Pr., Nissho	J	Tokyo, 10th meeting
2/28-4/9	LAFTA trends, econ. coop. heavy & chem. exports	Mizukami Tatsuzo Pr., Mitsui Trading	G	Trinidad-Tobago, Venezuela, Brazil, Uruguay, Paraguay, Argentina & New York, Washington
3	Doyukai joint res. on East-West Trade	NA	C	Doyukai, CED, and 5 groups from Western Europe
3/13 (4 wks)	Survey Aust.-NZ to increase Pacific trade	Ishizaka Rokuro Exec. Dir., Toshiba Machinery	G	Australia & New Zealand
5/4-5/13	J-Australia Joint Cmte.	Adachi Tadashi Pr., Nissho	J	Tokyo, 3d meeting. Discussed a Pacific org.

5	Doyukai joint res. on East-West Trade	NA	C	Brussels; 5 U.S., West European & Japanese groups issue joint policy statement
6/12-7/2	EEC discr. vs. Japanese goods	Ishizaka Taizo Pr., Keidanren	P	EEC members & Greece as assoc. member
6	Survey Sov. iron & steel industry	Nagano Shigeo Pr., Fuji Iron & Steel	P	Moscow; Agreed to Soviet proposal for Joint Econ. Cmte. from 1966
8	Econ. coop—giving & receiving	Kitazawa Kazue Pr., Sumitomo Elec.; Nakayama Sohei Pr., Indust. Bank of J	P	Central & South America & AID, CED, IBRD in U.S.
8/24-9/16	Talks w/top Sov. officials on trade and coop.	Uemura Kogoro VP, Keidanren	G	USSR, 8 cities
8/28-9/30	Survey new African markets	Echigo Masakazu Ch., C. Itoh Trading	G	Ethiopia, Zambia, Congo, Nigeria, Ivory Coast, Senegal
9/7-9/21	L-T trade agreement	Okazaki Kaheita Pr., All Nippon Air	P	Signed fiscal '66 terms w/Cm. China
9	Doyukai joint res. on Phil., Thai., E-W trade	Ibuka Masaru Pr., Sony	C	Melbourne, 2d meeting w/CED and CEDA
9/21-9/22	J-UK Businessmen's Conf.	Adachi Tadashi Pr., Nissho; Uemura Kogoro VP, Keidanren	C	Tokyo, 1st meeting: under Keidanren & Confed. of Br. Industries
10/19-10/20	J-U.S. Businessmen's Conf.	Takasugi Shinichi Adv., Mitsubishi Elec.	C	Chicago, 4th meeting; Keidanren & U.S. Natl. Ch. of Commerce
10/28-10/30	J-Calif. Assoc.	Iwasa Yoshizane Pr., Fuji Bank	C	Ito, 1st meeting; org. by individuals, Japan & U.S. West Coast
11	Doyukai joint res. on "econ devel. of less devel. counts."	NA	C	Paris, 7 Japanese, U.S. & West European groups on proposal by CEPES

(continued)

Appendix A (continued)

Date	Purpose	Chairman	Type	Remarks
11/16-11/22	J-Canada Businessmen's Conf.	Uemura Kogoro VP, Keidanren	C	Tokyo, 3d meeting
11/30-12	Nat'l devel. plans in Near & Mid. East	Horie Shigeo Pr., Bank of Tokyo	G	Afghanistan, Iran, Iraw, Kuwait, Saudi Arabia, Turkey; 1st regional govt. mission to this region
		1966		
1/19-2/26	Survey EEC-Africa affiliation	Tanibayashi Masatoshi Controller, Mitsubishi Trading	G	Senegal, Mali, Ivory Coast, Togo, Dahomey, Cameroons, Gabon, Chad, France, Germany, Belgium
1/27-2/5	Discuss a joint bus. coop. cmte. w/India	Adachi Tadashi Pr., Nissho	P	Agreed to estab. joint cmte.
2	Doyukai joint res. on "econ. devel. of less devel. countrs."	NA	C	7 Japanese, U.S., West European groups on proposal by CEPES
2/18-2/23	J-ROK Joint Econ. Conf.	Ishizaka Taizo Pr., Keidanren	C	Tokyo, 1st meeting; Discussed econ. coop., indust. technology, trade
2/18-3/16	Survey Caribbean econ. & devel. plans	Emori Morihisa Exec. dir., Mitsubishi Trading	G	Mexico, Ecuador, El Salvador, Guatemala, Dominican Republic, Jamaica, Puerto Rico
2/28-3/22	Extend ties w/US W. Coast	Hiyama Hiro Pr., Marubeni Iida	G	California, Oregon, Arizona, Washington
3/10-3/11	J-Argentine Joint Cmte.	Adachi Tadashi Pr., Nissho	J	Tokyo, 1st meeting
3/12-3/23	J-Soviet Joint Cmte.	Adachi Tadashi Pr., Nissho	J	Tokyo, 1st meeting

Date	Activity	Name / Title		Notes
3 (3wks)	Survey LAFTA progress	Yamanaka Hiroshi Exec. dir., Meiji Life	G	Mexico, Peru, Chile, Argentina, Brazil, Uruguay
4/11- 4/12	J-Mexico Econ. Council	Inagaki Heitaro Pr., J. For. Trade Council	C	Tokyo, 2d meeting; Called for both govts. to conclude try. of commerce and nav.
4/19- 4/21	J-Australia Joint Cmte.	Adachi Tadashi Pr., Nissho	J	Canberra, 4th meet. Canada & New Zealand observers for PBECC discuss.
5/5- 5/6	J-France Joint Econ. Cmte.	Ishizaka Taizo Pr., Keidanren	J	Paris, 1st meeting; trade issues
7	Doyukai joint res. on "econ. devel. of developing counts."	NA	C	7 Japanese U.S. & West European groups on proposal by CEPES
7	Doyukai joint res. on Phil., Thai. case studies	Yamashita Seiichi Exec. Secy., Doyukai	C	Melbourne, 3d meeting; Doyukai, CED, CEDA
9/3- 9/25	Survey Soviet Far East & Siberia	Arai Yuzo Pr., Dowa Mining	G	2d govt. mission to USSR
10/1- 11/1	Survey EEC, EFTA agriculture policy	Tohata Shiro Dir. gen., Agr., Res. Cmte.	G	Denmark, Belgium, United Kingdom, West Germany, France, Netherlands, Switzerland, Italy
10/3- 10/	Goodwill w/Korea	Adachi Tadachi Pr., Nissho	P	ROK, primarily Chambers of Comm.
10	"Modernization of indust. system in Eur. countries"	Oya Shinzo Pr., Teijin	P	United Kingdom, France, Belgium, West Germany
10	Doyukai joint res. on "econ devel. of developing counts."	NA	C	7 Japanese, U.S. & West European groups on proposal by CEPES

(continued)

Appendix A (continued)

Date	Purpose	Chairman	Type	Remarks
10/27-10/29	Cmte. for Prom. of Taiwan-J Coop.	Adachi Tadashi Pr., Nissho	J	7 Taipei, 11th meeting
11/1-12/8	Survey Near & Mid. East devel., monetary conds. & trade	Yamamoto Yoshio Exec. dr., C. Itoh Trading	G	Kuwait, Saudi Arabia, Bahrein, Kataru, Torusharu States, Aden, Yemen, United Arab Republic
11/3-11/5	J-Calif. Assoc.	Iwasa Yoshizane Pr., Fuji Bank	C	Palm Desert, Calif. Broad agenda incl. trade w/com. bloc
12	Doyukai joint res. on "econ devel. of developing counts."	NA	C	7 Japanese, U.S. & West European groups on proposal by CEPES
		1967		
2-3	Econ. coop. w/devel. countries of Africa	Kitazawa Kazue Pr., Sumitomo Elec.	P	Kenya, Uganda, Tanzania, Malawi, Zambia, Nigeria, Ethiopia
2/26-3/26	Survey infl. of industrialization, Viet. War & Cm. China's products in SE Asia	Honda Eiji Man. Dir., Sumitomo Trading	G	Thailand, Malaysia, Singapore, Hong Kong, Taiwan
3/14-3/15	J-ROK Econ. Conf.	Uemura Kogoro VP, Keidanren	C	Seoul, 2d meeting; On technology, econ. coop., trade
3/22-4/4	Economic mission to Pakistan	Doko Toshio Pr., Toshiba	G	East & West Pakistan
4/2-5/1	J-Australia Bus. Coop. Cmte.	Adachi Tadashi Pr., Nissho	J	Tokyo, 5th meeting
4/26-4/27	Pacific Basin Econ. Coop. Cmte.	Nagano Shigeo Pr., Fuji Iron & Steel	J	Tokyo, organizational meeting, incl. Japanese, Australian, New Zealand & U.S., and Canadian obsvs.
6/7-6/20	J-Soviet Joint Econ. Cmte.	Nagano Shigeo Pr., Fuji Iron & Steel	J	Moscow, 2d meeting

Dates	Organization	Representative	Code	Notes
6/10–6/30	J-Midwest Trade & contacts	Kikawada Kazutaka, Pr., Tokyo Elec. Power	G	U.S. Midwest, esp. Chicago; led to J-Midwest Assoc.
6	Doyukai joint res. on "econ. devel. of devel. countries"	NA	C	London, final meet. w/joint decl. on trade policy (7 grps.)
9/12–9/20	J-India Business Coop. Cmte.	Adachi Tadashi, Pr., Nissho	J	Tokyo, 1st meeting
9/27–10/3	J-Canada Businessmen's Conf.	Nagano Shigeo, Pr., Fuji Iron & Steel	C	Montreal, 4th meeting
10/5–10/7	J-Calif. Assoc.	Iwasa Yoshizane, Pr., Fuji Bank	C	Shima, 3d meeting
10/10–10/14	J-UK Businessmen's Conf.	Ishizaka Taizo, Pr., Keidanren	C	London, 2d meeting; J. explained PBEC.
10/12–11/5	Survey J. emigrants & trade prospects in C & S Amer.	Kobayashi Ataru, Pr., Arabian Oil	A	Mexico, Venezuela, Peru, Argentina, Paraguay, Brazil, United States
10/20–10/24	J-Argentina Joint Econ. Cmte.	Adachi Tadashi, Pr., Nissho	J	Buenos Aires, 2d meeting. Discussed specific trade items
10/24–10/25	Cmte. for Prom. of Taiwan-J Coop., econ. section meet.	Horikoshi Teizo, Dir. Gen., Keidanren	J	Tokyo, 12th meeting
10/28–11/5	J-France Joint Econ. Cmte.	Ishizaka Taizo, Pr., Keidanren	J	Tokyo, 2d meeting
11/1–11/2	J-Midwest Econ. Conf.	Kikawada Kazutaka, Pr., Tokyo Elec. Power	C	Hakone, 1st meeting; U.S. led by Pr., Chicago Assoc. of Comm. & Industry
11/13–11/17	J-U.S. Businessmen's Conf.	Ishizaka Taizo, Pr., Keidanren	C	Tokyo, 5th meeting; U.S. accepts J. invitation to join PBEC

(continued)

Appendix A (continued)

Date	Purpose	Chairman	Type	Remarks
11/20-11/21	J-W. Ger. businessmen's conf.	Uemura Kogoro VP., Keidanren	C	Tokyo, 1st conf. Germany accepts J. prop. for J-Ger. Joint Cmte.
12	Doyukai joint conf. on "non-tariff barriers"	Mizusawa Kenzo NA	C	Stockholm, 1st meet. 7 Japanese, U.S., West European groups
1968				
1/19-2/21	Capital liberalization reactions in W. Eur. & Canada	Ihara Ryu Pr., Yokohama Bank	G	France, West Germany, Italy, Belgium, Netherlands, United Kingdom, Switzerland, Sweden, Austria, Canada
2/13-2/17	J-ROK Econ. Conf.	Ishizaka Taizo Pr., Keidanren	G	Tokyo, 3d meeting
2	PBEC directors meeting	Nagano Shigeo Pr., Fuji Iron & Steel	J	Honolulu; to decide agenda for general meeting
3	Doyukai joint res. SE Asia development aid	Kikawada Kazutaka Pr., Tokyo Elec. Power	C	Tokyo, specialists of Doyukai, CED, CEDA
3/17-3/28	Lobby vs. proposed U.S. import surcharge	Sato Kiichiro Ch., Mitsui Bank	P	Washington, D.C.; New York
3/25-4/18	Survey economies of E. Europe	Iida Yoshizane V. Ch., Sov-E. Eur. Trade Assoc.	G	Hungary, Czechoslovakia, Yugoslavia
5/6-5/8	J-Australia Bus. Coop. Cmte.	Adachi Tadashi Pr., Nissho	J	Canberra, 6th meeting; timed w/PBEC meet. in Sydney
5/9-5/10	Pacific Basin Econ. Coop. Cmte.	Nagano Shigeo Pr., Fuji Iron & Steel	J	Sydney, 1st general meeting
7/9-7/10	Doyukai Conf. on "non-tariff barriers"	Mizusawa Kenzo NA	C	West Germany, 2d meeting, 7 Japanese, U.S., West European groups

122

Date	Event	Person		Location / Notes
9/20-9/22	J-Calif. Assoc.	Iwasa Yoshizane Pr., Fuji Bank	C	Monterey-Del Monte, 4th meeting
9/21-10/11	Direct invest. & techn. assistance	Hasegawa Norishige Pr., Sumitomo Chem.	G	Brazil, Mexico
9/23-9/24	PBEC directors meeting	Nagano Shigeo Pr., Fuji Iron & Steel	J	Honolulu; Japan, United States, Australia, New Zealand, Canada
9/29-10/9	Indonesian devel. plans & J's role	Takasugi Shinichi Advisor, Mitsubishi Elec.	G	Indonesia. Talks w/Suharto incl. Iwasa, Nagano, Doko
10/7-10/9	Cmte. for Prom. of Taiwan-J. Coop.	Adachi Tadashi Pr., Nissho	J	Taipei, 13th gen. meeting. Kishi an advisor & speaker
10/28-10/29	J-France Joint Econ. Cmte.	Ishizaka Taizo Pr., EXPO 70	J	Paris, 3d meeting
10/30	Informal talks w/ Austrian ldrs.	Nakayama Sohei Ch., Indust. Bank of J.	P	Vienna; Austrian stopover en route to conf. in West Germany
11/4	Doyukai-W. Ger. Conf. on post-Vietnam pd.	Kikawada Kazutaka Pr., Tokyo Elec. Power	C	Dusseldorf, West Germany Econ. & Social Devel. Cmte.
11/4-11/5	Expansion of J. imports, coop. w/Iran 5 yr. plan	Hirata Keiichiro Pr., Multipurpose Land Devel. Council	G	Teheran; follow up of MITI Min. Shiina visit of 10/13/68
11/5-11/10	More capital investment in India	Nagano Shigeo Pr., Fuji Iron & Steel	C	Bombay, incl. Mrs. Gandhi & External Affairs Minister
11/7-11/8	J-Italy Joint Econ. Cmte.	Doi Masaharu Ch., Sumitomo Chem.	J	Tokyo & Osaka, 3d meeting
11/18-11/21	J-ROK Trade Consultative Cmte.	Tanibayashi Masatoshi Mng. Dir., J. For. Trade Council	C	Seoul, 3d meeting
12/9-12/14	J-Soviet Joint Econ. Cmte.	Uemura Kogoro Pr., Keidanren	J	Tokyo, 3d meeting; Set up cmtes. of experts

Legend: NA, not available; A, roving ambassador; C, international businessmen's conference; J, joint economic committee; G, government sponsored mission; P, business sponsored mission. For acronyms of organizations, see List of Abbreviations.

Sources: Records and reports (see bibliography) of Keidanren and Keizai Doyukai; Keidanren Geppo; Keidanren Review; Ministry of Foreign Affairs, Waga gaiko no kinkyo (Tokyo: Finance Ministry, annual); newspapers; Japan Quarterly chronology section; "Kaigi haken keizai shisetsudanra hokokusho tenji mokuroku" [Catalog of reports on overseas economic missions and the like] (Tokyo: Keizai Dantai Rengokai, 1971).

APPENDIX B

Private Economic Diplomacy by Region and Country, 1956-68

(economic missions, roving ambassador appointments,
joint economic committee meetings, and international
businessmen's conferences)

Region and Country	Total	1956	1957	1958	1959	1960	1961	1962	1963	1964	1965	1966	1967	1968
Pacific Basin	58			2	1		5	5	3	6	10	8	9	9
United States	(38)			(1)	(1)		(3)	(4)	(1)	(4)	(7)	(7)	(6)	(4)
Canada	(10)			(1)			(2)	(2)	(1)	(1)	(1)		(1)	(1)
Australia	(13)			(1)			(1)		(1)	(2)	(3)	(2)	(1)	(2)
New Zealand	(3)			(1)			(1)				(1)			
Western Europe	44		1	1		1	1	4	5	5	6	8	5	7
Italy	(4)							(1)		(1)	(1)			(1)
United Kingdom	(3)							(1)			(1)		(1)	
France	(3)											(1)	(1)	(1)
Germany (Fed. Rep.)	(2)												(1)	(1)
Austria	(1)													(1)
Sweden	(1)													(1)
East Asia	29	1	2	2	2	2	2	3	2	1	2	3	4	3
Nationalist China	(15)		(2)	(1)	(2)		(2)	(1)	(1)	(1)	(1)	(1)	(2)	(1)
Korea (ROK)	(7)							(1)				(2)	(2)	(2)
Communist China	(6)	(1)				(2)		(1)	(1)		(1)			
Southeast Asia	14	4	1	2			1	1	1		2			1	1
Indonesia	(2)	(1)												(1)
Philippines	(2)	(2)												
Malaysia	(1)							(1)						
Vietnam (South)	(1)			(1)										
Burma	(1)					(1)								
Eastern Europe	11							2	1	1	2	2	1	2
USSR	(8)							(2)			(2)	(2)	(1)	(1)
South Asia	9		1	1	2					1		1	2	1
India	(3)											(1)	(1)	(1)
Pakistan	(2)				(1)							(1)		
Central America & Caribbean	9		1		1			2			1	2	1	1
Mexico	(3)							(1)				(1)		(1)
South America	9		1							1		2	2	1
Argentina	(2)											(1)	(1)	
Brazil	(1)													(1)
North Africa & Middle East	8		1			2	1			1	1	1		1
Iran	(2)					(1)								(1)
Africa	7					1	2		1		1	1	1	
Nigeria	(2)					(1)	(1)							
Ghana	(1)					(1)								
Mediterranean	1					1								
Total	199	5	8	8	6	8	12	17	13	17	25	28	26	26

Note: Missions, joint committee meetings, and conferences involving only one or two specific countries are listed in parentheses; these cases are also included in regional figures.

Sources: Official reports (Bibliography); Ministry of Foreign Affairs, Waga gaiko no kinkyo [Present state of our foreign relations] (Tokyo: Ministry of Finance, annual); Keizai Doyukai and Keidanren staff interviews and documents, particularly "Kaigi haken keizai shisetsudanra hokokuho tenji mokuroku" [Catalog of reports on overseas economic missions and the like] (Tokyo: Keizai Dantai Rengokai, 1971); Japanese and English language newspapers.

REPORTS*

"Dainiji Keizai Doyukai Oshu togo chosadan hokokusho" [Report of
the second Japan Committee for Economic Development survey
team on European integration]. Tokyo: Keizai Doyukai, May
1962.

"To Afurika haken keizai shisetsudan hokoku" [Report of the economic
mission to East Africa]. Tokyo: Economic Affairs Bureau,
Ministry of Foreign Affairs, June 1962.

"EEC to Nihon: EEC keizai chosadan hokokusho" [EEC and Japan:
Report of the economic survey team to the EEC]. Osaka:
Osaka Shoko Kaigisho, November 1962.

"Ho-I keizai shisetsudan hokokusho" [Report of the economic mission
to Italy]. Tokyo: Ho-I keizai shisetsudan, November 1962.

"Hō-O-Bei keizai shisetsudan hokokusho" [Report of the economic
mission to Europe and the United States]. Tokyo: Nihon Keizai
Chosa Kyogikai, January 1963.

"Ho EEC keizai shisetsudan hokokusho" [Report of the economic
mission to the EEC]. Tokyo: Keizai Dantai Rengokai, April
1963.

"Mareishia to no keizai kyoryoku: ho Mareishia keizai chosadan
hokokusho" [Economic cooperation with Malaysia: report of
the economic survey team to Malaysia]. Tokyo: Keizai Dantai
Rengokai, June 1963.

_____

*Reports are listed by year of publication; other sections of
the bibliography are in alphabetical order by author. Most of the
reports are available at the Keidanren library in Tokyo. See "Kaigai
haken keizai shisetsudanra hokokusho tenji mokuroku" [Catalog of
reports on overseas economic missions and the like] (Tokyo: Keizai
Dantai Rengokai, 1971). SRI reports are available at the library of
Stanford Research Institute, Menlo Park, California.

"To-O boeki shisetsudan hokokusho" [Report of the trade mission to Eastern Europe]. Tokyo: Ministry of Foreign Affairs, December 1963.

"Andesu shokoku boeki shisetsudan hokokusho" [Report of the trade mission to various countries of the Andes]. Tokyo: Economic Affairs Bureau, Ministry of Foreign Affairs, December 1963.

"Daisanji Oshu keizai togo chosandan hokokusho" [Report of the third survey team on European economic integration]. Tokyo: Keizai Doyukai, January 1964.

"Dainikai Nikka jitsugyojin kaigi Nihon daihyodan hokokusho" [Report of the Japanese delegation to the second Japan-Canada business-men's conference]. Tokyo: Keizai Dantai Rengokai, February 1964.

"Ho-O keizai shisetsudan hokokusho" [Report of the economic mission to Europe]. Tokyo: Economic Affairs Bureau, Ministry of Foreign Affairs, March 1964.

"Kita Afurika keizai shisetsudan hokokusho" [Report of the economic mission to North Africa]. Tokyo: Economic Affairs Bureau, Ministry of Foreign Affairs, March 1964.

"1964 nen ho-Bei keizai shisetsudan hokokusho" [Report of the 1964 economic mission to the United States]. Tokyo: 1964 nen ho-Bei keizai shisetsudan, October 1964.

"Report of the 1964 Japanese Economic Mission to the United States." Tokyo: 1964 nen ho-Bei keizai shisetsudan, 1964.

"Showa 39 nendo Oshu keizai togo chosa cheemu hokokusho" [Report of the 1964 survey team on European economic integration]. Tokyo: Economic Affairs Bureau, Ministry of Foreign Affairs, January 1965.

"Ho-Ka keizai shisetsudan hokokusho" [Report of the economic mission to Canada]. Tokyo: Ho-Ka keizai shisetsudan, January 1965.

"Sei-O shokoku no teikaihatsukoku keizai kyoryoku: dainiji Oshu keizai shisetsudan hokokusho" [Economic cooperation with the developing countries of Western Europe: report of the second economic mission to Europe]. Tokyo: Nihon Seisansei Honbu, March 1965.

"1965 nen Nanbei keizai shisetsudan hokokusho" [Report of the 1965 economic mission to South America]. Tokyo: 1965 nen Nanbei keizai shisetsudan, October 1965.

"Ho EEC keizai shisetsudan hokokusho" [Report of the economic mission to the EEC]. Tokyo: Keizai Dantai Rengokai, December 1965.

"Nikka kyoryoku iinkai dai 11 kai sokai kiroku" [Record of the 11th general meeting of the Committee for the Promotion of Taiwan-Japanese Cooperation]. Tokyo: Nikka Kyoryoku Iinkai, 1966.

"Chukinto keizai shisetsudan hokokusho" [Report of the economic mission to the Near and Middle East]. Tokyo: Kukiuto Keizai Shisetsudan, May 1966.

"EEC rengo Afurika shokoku chosandan no kaidanroku" [Discussion report of the survey team to countries of the EEC and Africa]. Tokyo: Economic Affairs Bureau, Ministry of Foreign Affairs, May 1966.

"Henbo suru To Europpa: Nihon seifu haken ho To-O keizai shisetsudan hokokusho" [Changing Eastern Europe: report of the government sponsored economic mission to Eastern Europe]. Tokyo: Keizai Dantai Rengokai, June 1966.

"Dai 4 kai Nichi-Go keizai godo iinkai kaigi kiroku" [Record of the fourth conference of the Japan-Australia Joint Economic Committees]. Tokyo: Nichi-Go Keizai Iinkai, July 1966.

"Dai 1 kai Nichi-Futsu keizai godo iinkai gijiroku" [Proceedings of the first meeting of the Japan-France Joint Economic Committees]. Tokyo: Nichi-Futsu Keizai Iinkai, July 1966.

"Seifu haken ho-So keizai shisetsudan hokokusho" [Report of the government economic mission to the USSR]. Tokyo: Keizai Dantai Rengokai, July 1966.

"Ho-Bei keizai shisetsudan hokokusho" [Report of the economic mission to the United States]. Tokyo: Ho-Bei Keizai Shisetsudan, September 1966.

"Ho-Kan shinzen Keizai shisetsudan hokokusho" [Report of the economic goodwill mission to Korea]. Tokyo: Nihon Shoko Kaigisho, October 1966.

"The Sydney Report." SRI International, Number Two, 1967.

"The Djakarta Report." SRI International, Number Three, 1967.

"Shiberia · Kyokuto kaihatsu to Nichi-So keizai koryu: Seifu haken dainiji keizai shisetsudan hokoku" [Siberia-Far East development and Japan-Soviet economic exchange: report of the second government sponsored economic mission]. Tokyo: Keizai Dantai Rengokai, March 1967.

"Siefu haken Tonan Ajia keizai chosadan hokokusho" [Report of the government economic survey team to Southeast Asia]. Tokyo: Tonan Ajia Keizai Chosadan, May 1967.

"Dai 5 kai Nichi-Go keizai godo iinkai kaigi kiroku" [Record of the 5th conference of the Japan-Australia Joint Economic Committees]. Tokyo: Nichi-Go Keizai Iinkai, October 1967.

"Taiheiyo keizai iinkai kaigi kiroku—setsuritsu kaigi" [Record of the founding conference, Pacific Basin Economic Committee]. Tokyo: Taiheiyo Keizai Iinkai, October 1967.

"Nichi-So, So-Nichi keizai iinkai dainikai godoiinkaigi hokokusho" [Report of the second joint committee meeting of the Japan-USSR and USSR-Japan Economic Committees]. Tokyo: Nisso Keizai Iinkai, November 1967.

"Dai 4 kai Nikka jitsugyojin kaigi hokokusho" [Report of the fourth Japan-Canada businessmen's conference]. Tokyo: Keizai Dantai Rengokai, December 1967.

"Kobayashi Ataru taishi ikko no Chunanbei 6 ka koku shuccho hokoku" [Report of Ambassador Ataru Kobayashi and his delegation to six countries of Central and South America]. Tokyo: Central and South American Emigration Bureau, Ministry of Foreign Affairs, December 1967.

"Dainikai Nichi-Ei zaikaijin kaigi hokokusho" [Report of the second Japan-United Kingdom businessmen's conference]. Tokyo: Keizai Dantai Rengokai, January 1968.

"Ho Bei keizai shisetsudan kaku kaidan kiroku" [Complete conference record of the economic mission to the United States]. Tokyo: Secretariat of the Economic Mission to the United States, April 1968.

"Sydney Meeting, Pacific Basin Committee. A Report on the First General Meeting—May 9-10, 1968." SRI International, Number Six, 1968.

"Japanese Government Economic Mission to the Republic of Indonesia, September 29-October 9, 1968." Tokyo: Ho-Indoneshia Keizai Shisetsudan, 1968.

"The Japan-California Association Report." SRI International, Number Thirteen, 1969.

"Seifu haken ho-Indoneshia keizai shisetsudan hokokusho" [Report of the government sponsored economic mission to Indonesia]. Tokyo: Ho-Indoneshia Keizai Shisetsudan, 1969.

"Nihon Karifuoruniya Kai dai 5 kai Nichi Bei godo kaigi gijiroku" [Proceedings of the fifth Japan-United States joint conference, Japan-California Association]. Tokyo: Nihon Karifuoruniya Kai, April 1970.

ARTICLES

Aichi, Kiichi. "Japan's Legacy and Destiny of Change." Foreign Affairs 48 (October 1969): 21-38.

Almond, Gabriel A. "The Politics of German Business." In West German Leadership and Foreign Policy. Edited by Hans Speir and W. Phillips Davison. Evanston, Ill.: Row, Peterson & Co., 1957, pp. 195-241.

"Asia-Pacific Economic Sphere: A Step Toward Realization." Asia Scene, March 1968, pp. 10-11.

Curtis, Gerald L. "Organizational Leadership in Japan's Economic Community." Journal of International Affairs 26 (1972): 179-85.

Fujii, Motohide. "Economic Diplomacy Makes Headway." Asia Scene, October 1963, pp. 6-9.

Fukui, Haruhiro. "The Associational Basis of Decision-Making in the Liberal-Democratic Party." In Research School of Pacific Studies, Papers on Modern Japan, 1965. Canberra: Australian National University, 1965, pp. 18-33.

Hayashi, Shozo. "Nihon no pawa erito" [The power elite in Japan]. Chuo Koron, January 1960, pp. 146-57.

Ishida, Takeshi. "The Development of Interest Groups and the Pattern of Modernization in Japan." In Research School of Pacific Studies, Papers on Modern Japan, 1965. Canberra: Australian National University, 1965, pp. 1-17.

_____. "Pressure Groups in Japan." Journal of Social and Political Ideas in Japan 2 (December 1964): 108-11.

Ishikawa, Ichiro. "Mokuhyo wa Nihon no fukko" [The goal is Japan's recovery]. Ekonomisuto, 4-11 (January 1966), pp. 156-63.

Ito, Daiichi. "Keizai kanryo no kodo yoshiki" [Behavior of economic bureaucrats]. In Gendai Nihon no seito to kanryo. Edited by Nihon Seiji Gakkai. Tokyo: Iwanami Shoten, 1967, pp. 78-104.

Iwasa, Yoshizane. "The Free Economy and the U.S." Japan Quarterly 11 (October/December 1964): 423-26.

Kato, Hidetoshi. "Symposium '71 Japan" (Advertisement) Fortune, August 1971, p. 42.

Kawai, Yoshinari. "Japanese-Soviet Cooperation for Development of Siberia." In Japan's Industrial Role, 1968. Tokyo: Asahi Evening News, 1968, p. 20.

Kimura, Takeo. "Sanken" [Industrial Problems Research Society]. Chuo Koran, July 1971, pp. 166-96.

Kosaka, Masataka. "Japan's Post-war Foreign Policy." In Papers on Modern Japan, 1968. Edited by D. C. S. Sissons. Canberra: Australian National University, 1968, pp. 1-25.

Kotaka, Yasuo. "Opinions of the Japanese Top Company Executives on the Social Conditions Closely Relating to the Long-Range Development of Business and Industry." Keio Business Review 1 (1962): 23-47.

Koto, Rikuzo. "Siberian Development: A Joint Japanese-Soviet Venture." Asia Scene, February 1968, pp. 80-83.

Kunimoto, Yoshiro. "Siberian Prospect." Japan Quarterly 16 (July-September 1969): 337-43.

Langdon, Frank C. "Big Business Lobbying in Japan—The Case of Central Bank Reform." American Political Science Review 55 (September 1961): 527-38.

_____. "The Political Contributions of Big Business in Japan." Asian Survey 3 (October 1963): 465-73.

Mendel, Douglas H. Jr. "Perspectives on Japanese Foreign Policy." Monumenta Nipponica 21 (1966): 346-53.

Mihashi, Kokichi. "Indonijia enjo to zaikai" [Indonesian aid and big business]. Ekonomisuto, 29 (October 1968), pp. 56-60.

Miki, Yonosuke. "Zaikai-seiji kenkin no uchimaku" [The inside facts on business political contributions]. Chuo Koron, June 1963, pp. 102-11.

Misawa, Shigeo. "Seisaku kettei katei no gaikan [Outline of the policy-decision-making process]. In Gendai Nihon no seito to kanryo. Edited by Nihon Seiji Gakkai. Tokyo: Iwanami Shoten, 1967, pp. 5-33.

Mushakoji, Kinhide. "Thought and Behavior of Japanese Diplomats." Journal of Social and Political Ideas in Japan 4 (April 1966): 19-25.

Nagai, Yonosuke. "Structural Characteristics of Pressure Politics in Japan." Journal of Social and Political Ideas in Japan 2 (December 1964): 101-07.

Nagano, Shigeo. "The First General Meeting of the Pacific Basin Economic Cooperation Committee." Keidanren Review 9 (October 1968): 45-50.

"Russo-Japanese Trade." Japan Quarterly 14 (October-December 1967): 422-28.

Noguchi, Yuichiro. "Economic Nationalism." Journal of Social and Political Ideas in Japan 4 (August 1966): 94-99.

_____. "Trends in Thought Among Structural Reformists in Japanese Industry." Journal of Social and Political Ideas in Japan 5 (April 1967): 11-26.

_____ "Yotsu no keieisha dantai" [Four employers' associations].
Chuo Koron, October 1960, pp. 157-65.

Sakaguchi, Akira. "The Power of the Financial World in Politics."
Journal of Social and Political Ideas in Japan 2 (December 1964):
115-19.

Sato, Kiichiro, et al. "Minkan keizai gaiko no yakuwari to seika"
[The role and results of private economic diplomacy]. Keidanren Geppo, December 1967, pp. 1-17.

_____. "The Role of Private Economic Diplomacy." Keidanren
Review 8 (March 1968): 26-35.

Scalapino, Robert A. "The Foreign Policy of Modern Japan." In
Foreign Policy in World Politics. Edited by Roy C. Macridis,
2d ed. Englewood Cliffs, N.J.: Prentice-Hall, 1962, pp. 225-66.

"Seijishoku ga takamaru zaikai minkan gaiko" [Political coloring
deepens in private business diplomacy]. Keizai Tembo, 1
(October 1968), p. 19.

Soma, Masao. "The Roots of Political Corruption." Journal of Social
and Political Ideas in Japan 5 (April 1967): 1-10.

Soukup, James R. "Business Political Participation in Japan:
Continuity and Change." Studies on Asia, vol. 6. Edited by
Robert K. Sakai. Lincoln: University of Nebraska Press, 1965,
pp. 163-78.

_____ . "Comparative Studies in Political Finance: Japan."
Journal of Politics 25 (November 1963): 737-56.

"A Straight-from-the-Shoulder Japanese Reminder." Fortune, May
1964, p. 110.

Takasugi, Shinichi. "Economic Aid to Indonesia." In Japan's Industrial Role, 1968, Tokyo: Asahi Evening News, 1968, pp.
18-19.

Tiedemann, Arthur E. "Big Business and Politics in Prewar Japan."
Dilemmas of Growth in Prewar Japan. Edited by James W.
Morley. Princeton, N.J.: Princeton University Press, 1971,
pp. 267-316.

Trezise, Philip H. "The Realities of Japan-U.S. Economic Relations," Pacific Community 1 (April 1970): 353-68.

Ways, Max. "Why Japan's Growth is Different." Fortune, November 1967, p. 127.

BOOKS

Akimoto, Hideo. Keidanren [Federation of Economics Organizations]. Tokyo: Sekkasha, 1968.

Aonuma, Yoshimatsu. Nihon keieiso [The Japanese managerial class]. Tokyo: Nihon Keizai Shimbunsha, 1965.

Asahi Shimbun, ed. Asian Development After Vietnam. Tokyo: Asahi Shimbun, 1968.

Braunthal, Gerard. Federation of German Industry in Politics. Ithaca, N.Y.: Cornell University Press, 1965.

Dimock, Marshall E. The Japanese Technocracy: Management and Government in Japan. New York: Walker/Weatherhill, 1968.

Hellmann, Donald C. Japanese Domestic Politics and Foreign Policy: The Peace Agreement with the Soviet Union. Berkeley: University of California Press, 1969.

Hollerman, Leon. Japan's Dependence on the World Economy: The Approach Toward Economic Liberalization. Princeton, N.J.: Princeton University Press, 1969.

Hoshii, Iwao. The Dynamics of Japan's Business Evolution. Tokyo, Philadelphia: Orient/West, 1966.

Huh, Kyung-Mo. Japan's Trade in Asia. New York: Frederick A. Praeger, 1966.

Hunsberger, Warren S. Japan and the United States in World Trade. New York: Harper & Row, Council on Foreign Relations, 1964.

Japanese Government. Economic Planning Agency. New Long Range Economic Plan of Japan, 1961-1970. Tokyo: Japan Times, 1961.

Kajima, Morinosuke. Modern Japan's Foreign Policy. Tokyo: Charles E. Tuttle, 1969.

Kato, Yoshinori. Zaikai [Big business circles]. Tokyo: Kawade Shobo Shinsha, 1966.

Kojima, Kiyoshi, ed. Pacific Trade and Development. Tokyo: Japan Economic Research Center, 1968.

Komiya, Ryutaro, ed. Postwar Economic Growth in Japan. Translated by Robert Ozaki. Berkeley: University of California Press, 1966.

Lockwood, William W., ed. The State and Economic Enterprise in Japan. Princeton, N.J.: Princeton University Press, 1965.

Mannari, Hiroshi. Bijinesu Erito [Business elites]. Tokyo: Chuo Koronsha, 1965.

Marshall, Byron K. Capitalism and Nationalism in Prewar Japan. Stanford, Calif.: Stanford University Press, 1967.

Murai, Misao. Hyakunin no zaikaijin [One hundred big business-men]. Tokyo: Diamondosha, 1967.

Nakane, Chie. Tate shakai no ningen kankei [Human relationships in a vertical society]. Tokyo: Kodansha, 1967.

Okita, Saburo. Nihon keizai no bijion [A vision of the Japanese economy]. Tokyo: Diamondosha, 1968.

Olson, Lawrence. Japan in Postwar Asia. New York: Frederick A. Praeger. Council on Foreign Relations, 1970.

Osgood, Robert E., George R. Packard III, John H. Badgley. Japan and the United States in Asia. Baltimore, Md.: Johns Hopkins Press, 1968.

Research and Policy Committee. East-West Trade: A Common Policy for the West. New York: Committee for Economic Development in association with Keizai Doyukai, CEPES—the European Committee for Economic and Social Progress, 1965.

_____. Japan in the Free World Economy (With a Statement by Keizai Doyukai). New York: Committee for Economic Development, 1963.

Sahashi, Shigeru. Ishoku Kanryo [A unique bureaucracy]. Tokyo: Diamondosha, 1967.

Sakaguchi, Akira. Keieisha—gendai no pawa erito [Management—modern power elite]. Tokyo: Kawade Shobo, 1964.

Scalapino, Robert A. and Junnosuke Masumi. Parties and Politics in Contemporary Japan. Berkeley: University of California Press, 1962.

Sebald, William J., C. Nelson Spinks. Japan: Prospects, Options and Opportunities. Washington, D.C.: American Enterprise Institute for Public Policy Research, 1967.

Suzuki, Yukio. Gendai Nihon no kenryoku erito [The power elite of contemporary Japan]. Tokyo: Bansho Shobo, 1967.

_____. Seiji o ugokasu keieisha [Businessmen who influence government]. Tokyo: Nihon Keizai Shimbunsha, 1965.

Thayer, Nathaniel B. How the Conservatives Rule Japan. Princeton, N.J.: Princeton University Press, 1969.

Tsuneishi, Warren M. Japanese Political Style. New York: Harper & Row, 1966.

Ward, Robert E. Japan's Political System. Englewood Cliffs, N.J.: Prentice-Hall, 1967.

Watanuki, Joji. Nihon no seiji shakai [Japan's political society]. Tokyo: Tokyo Daigaku Shuppankai, 1967.

Yamamura, Kozo. Economic Policy in Postwar Japan. Berkeley: University of California Press, 1967.

Yanaga, Chitoshi. Big Business in Japanese Politics. New Haven, Conn.: Yale University Press, 1968.

Yoshino, M. Y. Japan's Managerial System. Cambridge: MIT Press, 1968.

UNPUBLISHED MATERIAL

Hoshii, Iwao. "The State and Business in Japan." Mimeographed. New York: Committee for Economic Development, December 1964.

McGarry, James F. "A Study of Decision-making in Japan's Postwar Foreign Economic Policy." Ph.D. dissertation, University of Pennsylvania, 1964.

INTERVIEWS

Arnold, Anthony, Second Secretary, Political Section, U.S. Embassy, Tokyo. 26 February 1969.

Dutton, Lawrence W. Second Secretary, Economic Section, U.S. Embassy, Tokyo. 26 February 1969.

Fujiwara, Katsuhiro. U.S.-Japan Trade Council. 19 January 1973.

Fusano, Natsuaki. Conference Planning Department, Keidanren. 30 October 1968.

Gibson, Dr. Weldon B. Executive Vice-President, Stanford Research Institute, and President, SRI International. 6 November 1971.

Gregory, John M. Second Secretary, Economic Section, U.S. Embassy, Tokyo. 12 September 1968 and 26 February 1969.

Hiroshima, Koji. Assistant to the President, Marubeni-Iida Co., Ltd. 6 March 1969.

Hiyama, Hiro. President, Marubeni-Iida Co., Ltd. 6 March 1969.

Iwasa, Yoshizane. President, The Fuji Bank, Ltd. 26 February 1969.

Kikawada, Kazutaka. President, Tokyo Electric Power Co., Inc. 7 March 1969.

Kondo, Yutaka. Economic Affairs Bureau, Ministry of Foreign Affairs. 1 July 1968.

Levin, Herbert. Second Secretary, Political Section, U.S. Embassy, Tokyo. 13 September 1968.

Makita, Harutsugu. Vice-President, Private Investment Company for Asia. 5 March 1969.

Makita, Yoichiro. Executive Vice-President, Mitsubishi Heavy Industries. 21 February 1969.

Marsh, Donald R. Vice-President, Morgan Guaranty Trust Company. 16 November 1972.

Miyazawa, Kiichi. Member of the Diet and Director General, Economic Planning Agency. 10 March 1969.

Mlynarchik, Roy. Chief, Translation Section, U.S. Embassy, Tokyo. 13 September 1968.

Muramatsu, Masami. Executive Director, Simul International. 20 February 1969.

Murazumi, Yasu. Economic Affairs Bureau, Ministry of Foreign Affairs. 1 August 1968.

Nagano, Shigeo. President, Fuji Iron and Steel Co., Ltd. 4 March 1969.

Nirasawa, Yoshio. Deputy Secretary-General, Keizai Doyukai. 13 July 1968.

Okabe, Kunio. Assistant General Manager, Foreign Affairs Department, Yawata Iron and Steel Co. 1 and 5 March 1969.

Okazaki, Hisahiko. Chief, Analysis Section, Ministry of Foreign Affairs. 1 July 1968.

Okita, Saburo. President, Japan Economic Research Center. 17 February 1969.

Omi, Koji. Consul, Consulate-General of Japan, New York. 31 January 1973.

Saeki, Muneyoshi. Former Member of the Diet. 22 February 1969.

Saito, Akira. Political Reporter, Mainichi Shimbun. 24 February 1969.

Sasaki, Masaya. Manager, Foreign Relations Department, Fuji Iron and Steel Co., Ltd. 5 March 1969.

Sasaki, Michio. Research Assistant, Keidanren. 17 February 1969.

Segawa, Masahisa. Secretary to the President, The Fuji Bank, Ltd. 26 October 1968 and 21 February 1969.

Shibata, Masuo, International Trade Planning Section, Ministry of International Trade and Industry. 18 September 1968.

Shinozawa, Kyosuke. Economic Affairs Bureau, Ministry of Foreign Affairs. 29 October 1968.

Steffans, Dr. Carsten. Director, SRI-Japan. 7 March 1969.

Takashima, Setsuo. Chief, Heavy Industries Bureau, Ministry of International Trade and Industry. 18 September 1968.

Takeyama, Yasuo. Chief, Editorial Staff, Nihon Keizai Shimbun. 18 February 1969.

Taki, Takaaki. Manager, Foreign Trade Section, Tokyo Chamber of Commerce. 28 February 1969.

Tawara, Takao. Managing Director, Nippon Mining Co., Ltd. 19 February 1969.

Tezuka, Banzo. Executive Director, Tokyo Chamber of Commerce and Industry. 28 February 1969.

Tsuchiya, Takao. Advisor, Bank of Japan. 1 November 1968.

Ueda, Atsuo. Assistant to the Managing Director, Keidanren. 20 September 1968, 17 February and 13 March 1969.

Yahagi, Seiichiro. Business Administration Division, The Fuji Bank, Ltd. 2 July 1968.

Yamada, Tadayoshi. Executive Director, Yawata Iron and Steel Co. 1 March 1969.

Yamashita, Seiichi. Secretary-General, Keizai Doyukai, 13 March 1969.

WILLIAM R. BRYANT is Senior Analyst for Utah International Inc., specializing in marketing for East Asia and the Pacific Basin. He has also served in a research capacity with the Social Science Research Council, Stanford Research Institute, and the International Affairs Seminars of Washington, with emphasis on Japanese business and government.

Dr. Bryant has done field work in Vietnam for AID and lived three years in Japan, in part as a faculty member at the University of Beppu.

Dr. Bryant holds degrees from the University of California at Berkeley, University of Hawaii, and a doctorate in political science from Columbia University.

RELATED TITLES
Published by
Praeger Special Studies

JAPAN: FINANCIAL MARKETS AND THE
WORLD ECONOMY
                    Wilbur R. Monroe

THE JAPANESE STEEL INDUSTRY: With an
Analysis of the U.S. Steel Import Problem
                    Kiyoshi Kawahito

MARKETING IN JAPAN: A Management Guide
                    Michael Y. Yoshino

TRAINING JAPANESE MANAGERS
                    Allen Dickerman